Unleashing India

Apsvantaramrutamapsu bheshaja |

— *Atharvaveda* (4/4)

Water is the elixir of life, water has medicinal value.

(Water is the primary necessity of the human body. Water is alike the elixir of life because of which the body is purified and we become energetic. Water also possesses medicinal value. It frees the body from different *doshas* [ailments] and is known as *bheshajya*. It gives us good health, happiness and contentment.)

Ta apaha Shiva apo ayakshmankaraniyaha |
Yathaiva tripyate mayastasta a datta bheshajihi ||

— *Atharvaveda* (2/5)

This water is beneficial to one and all, it cures all the ailments. Alike the happiness, which increases, that water is like a panacea for all the diseases, please accept it.

(The medicinal value and nobleness of water is omniscient. Water itself is alike a panacea to cure many a disease.)

Unleashing India

Water: Elixir of Life

Volume II

M. Veerappa Moily

Rupa . Co

Published 2009 by

Rupa . Co

7/16, Ansari Road, Daryaganj,
New Delhi 110 002

Sales Centres:

Allahabad Bengalooru Chandigarh Chennai
Hyderabad Jaipur Kathmandu
Kolkata Mumbai

Typeset by
Mindways Design
1410 Chiranjiv Tower
43 Nehru Place
New Delhi 110 019

Printed in India by
Rekha Printers Pvt Ltd.
A-102/1, Okhla Industrial Area, Phase-II,
New Delhi-110 020

Dedicated to
The Memory of Dr. Y.S. Rajasekhara Reddy
Who Ushered in a Revolution in Irrigation and
Drinking Water by Innovative Jala Yagna

*The earth has enough to meet the needs of everyone,
but not for their greed.*

Mahatma Gandhi

CONTENTS

Acknowledgements

I take this opportunity to thank my daughter Hamsa, my son Harsha and my wife Malathi for their immense support throughout.

I am grateful to Shri R.K. Singh, IAS, who has always been a strong pillar of support. Shri Nazir Husain, Former Director (Planning), Government of Karnataka has taken lot of efforts to compile the data and also provided the research input. Ms Mahua Moitra and Shri S.K. Das, IAS (retd) former Secretary, Government of Karnataka and Director (Finance), ISRO, Bangalore and also Professor Prakash, Agriculture University, Bangalore have taken pains to edit the draft.

The following persons rendered valuable inputs to present this volume: Shri Chiranjiv Singh, IAS (retd.), former Additional Chief Secretary and Development Commissioner, Government of Karnataka; Dr Vasanth Kumar, Director of Horticulture, Government of Karnataka; Shri Vijaykumar Gogi, IFS, Project Officer (Forestry), Biomass Energy for Rural India Project, Bangalore; and Shri H.V. Janardhan, Deputy Director of Agriculture (retd.), Department of Agriculture, Government of Karnataka.

Foreword

Conserving Water to Make Every Drop Matter

Water is life and becoming ever more precious as population and demands grow. Pollution and, now, global warming have enhanced water stress and India and its northwestern, western and southern regions are becoming more vulnerable to the vagaries of the monsoon. At a time when we need to re-educate ourselves about the new realities and imperatives of our water future, it is a matter for satisfaction that a political personality of stature like Dr M. Veerappa Moily, currently Union Law Minister, should take time to address this critical issue in the *Unleashing India – Water: Elixir of Life*.

Dr Moily comes to the task with an abundance of experience as a political leader, former Chief Minister of Karnataka and, more recently, as Chairman of the Administrative Reforms Commission which has just concluded its monumental labours. The ARC did not directly address water issues, but the topic is so ubiquitous that the subject kept creeping into the narrative under a variety of headings including such things as NREGA, with rural employment oriented towards maintaining and improving local water assets, disaster management (flood and drought), environmental sustainability and conflict resolution.

The message of the book is taken from Gandhi's text that there is enough for everyone's need but not enough for everybody's greed, which translates into waste not, want not. India is a wasteful user of water on account of overuse, resulting in waterlogging and salinity for lack of drainage, low or non-pricing of water, so that an essentially scarce resource is treated as a free good, and poor maintenance leading to asset deterioration. Dr Moily's message is, therefore, that water must be treated as a public trust. The corollary then must be that those responsible for the stewardship of the nation's water resources are not merely managers but public trustees of the greater common good.

Though water has a multitude of uses and functions, the largest quantum goes to irrigation to sustain the nation's food supply. Though the percentage of utilisable water devoted to non-agricultural uses is rising with population growth (drinking water and municipal supplies), industrialisation, recreation and ecological uses, agriculture still remains and will always remain by far the largest user in the prevailing tropical conditions. Yet nutritional levels in India are unacceptably low and a far larger agricultural output is required to provide the food, feed, fibre and seed for a growing population that has multiplied almost threefold since Independence and will grow by another 1.5 times of India-1947 to stabilise around 1650 million within the next forty years.

This is Dr Moily's concern. How do we 'stretch' our finite water resources to meet pressing new demands and feed growing numbers? Smaller nations can import food, but this can only be an emergency and marginal option for a huge country like India, a sixth of all mankind, which could itself absorb almost all of the world's surplus grain reserves (if this were affordable and politically feasible), leaving nothing for other food importers. The greater part of India's farmlands are still rain fed, despite the fact that it is today the world's largest irrigator (almost 100 m hectares (gross potential) as against an outer irrigation potential of 140 m ha with trans-basin transfers (inter-linking of rivers).

Most irrigation is by groundwater, which is more cost effective as it is micro-managed by users who own the source, though not the resource. But this is poor comfort in a larger context as surface and groundwater are part of the same hydrological cycle. The quantum of groundwater can be enhanced by watershed management and other forms of recharge. But Dr Moily's strategy is to get more crop per drop. To this end he advocates maximising water saving methods of irrigation such as drip and sprinkler which have already gained vogue in parts of the country but hold much promise elsewhere. Small farmers can resort to these systems through cooperative or contractual means and while significant capital and energy costs may have to be incurred, the resultant gains are likely to be far greater.

Even so, such methods are currently more suited to horticulture, vegetable and other garden crops and are less viable in the case of paddy and wheat which are water intensive and grown over vast acreages. Results for sugarcane appear promising according to Dr Moily's findings. Diversification that ensures more cost-effective and ecologically sound cropping patterns, would seem the better alternative together with resort to newer varieties that demand less water or are salt tolerant. Improved tillage practices such as mulching and the System of Rice Intensification (SRI) also offer higher crop-water returns.

There are four other aspects of water management that one hopes Dr Moily will address in his future writings. The first of these is climate change and what we need to do o adjust to the new hydrology this creates. The second is regional cooperation in harnessing the waters of the Indus, Ganges and Brahmaputra/Meghna, all of which are international rivers. Optimal development calls for cooperation as the actions of and impacts on upper and lower riparians cannot be ignored as they have basin-wide implications. Further, many national solutions will be found in international collaboration. The third relates to the excessive classification of water-related and cartographic data which has emerged as a huge impediment to purposeful thinking and planning at every level. Of this, Dr Moily has written elsewhere in one of his ARC reports. Finally, rivers carve out natural resource regions that do not coincide with administrative and political boundaries in our federal set up. Dr Moily refers to river boards and basin authorities. But these constitutional provisions have remained politically unacceptable. Hence the need to look at water markets, water parliaments and other innovative measures to bridge the divide. With his vast experience in administrative reforms and as Law Minister, this is an area of reform that Dr Moily is well placed to put on the national agenda and carry forward the debate on how these important issues may best be addressed.

This will go well with the larger canvas of *Unleashing India – Water: Elixir of Life* within which Dr Moily looks at meeting India's looming water needs.

B.G. Verghese
Former Editor, *Indian Express*

Preface

'Air is the Guru, Water is the Father, and Earth is the Great Mother of all.'

– *Guru Granth Sahib*

The preamble of the White Paper on Water Policy of South Africa of 30 April 1993 says 'Water is a basic human right and the giver of life'. It quotes poet Mazisi Kunene 'From water is born all people of the earth'. It is also said that status of the nation's water resource is an individual asset, and national government will act as the custodian of the nation's water resources and it will be operated as a people's trust.

The time has come for India to revisit our water policies and redesign them in the national interest with the focus on treating water resources and its use to be exercised as a 'public trust'.

There are two fundamental issues: First, the overexploitation of groundwater, and second, poor prioritisation of government spending – over 60% of its resources goes into budgeting for large dam and canal projects, without making sure that gains from these are optimised. Meanwhile, existing infrastructure gathers silt deposits and cannot store to its full potential and many a time, it is old and leakages lead to a lot of wastage.

Groundwater is, in fact, India's lifeline – it feeds an estimated two-thirds of all irrigated foodgrain-producing farmland, provides most of the rural drinking water and half of all urban and industrial use. But groundwater is often over-exploited – which means more water is drawn on average than is replenished by rain.

Local community-level responsibility in managing groundwater resources is one pragmatic solution. Unfortunately, provisions under the 73rd amendment of the Constitution to hand water management to panchayats, have not even been implemented, leave alone made effective. But we cannot afford not to take up the challenging task of dealing with the water constraint any longer.

Even sixty years after Independence, 60% of the farm lands are still dependent on monsoons. Efforts to increase the area under irrigation in the past decade have been an abysmal failure. Between 1981 and 1991 the annual growth of land being brought under irrigation was 2.27%. But between 1991 and 2004, that figure dropped to 1.15%. In real terms, between 1985 and 1995, 14 lakh hectares were brought under irrigation. But between 1995 and 2005 that figure fell to 6.85 lakh hectare.

There was a major slow-down in investment in infrastructure for agriculture in the past decade. Public investment in irrigation has declined from 23% of the total plan outlay in the First Plan period to 5% in the Tenth Five Year Plan (FYP).

Even the figure of 6.8 lakh hectare of additional land brought under irrigation during the past decade is disputed by the Planning Commission. It commented that the landuse data shows no real increase in irrigated area. Strangely, for the tenth Plan, while the target of spending Rs 90,000 crore towards investment in irrigation was met, the potential added was only half of the stated figure of 16 million hectare. Meanwhile, there are some 480-odd irrigation projects that need to be completed apart from 240 new ones being proposed.

In Karnataka, groundwater levels were depleting at an alarming rate of 70 cm a year. In Uttar Pradesh, three years of drought has brought farmers to their knees.

Analysing the countrywise geographical area, arable land and irrigated area in the world, it is found that among the continents, largest geographical area lies in Africa which is about 23% of the world geographic area. However, Asia (excluding erstwhile countries of USSR) with only 21% of world geographical area has about 32% of world's arable land followed by North Central America having about 20% of world's arable land. Africa has only 12% of world's arable land. It has been seen that irrigated area in the world is 18.5% of the arable land in 1994. In 1989, 63% of world's irrigated area was in Asia, whereas in 1994 this percentage has gone up to 64%. Also, 37% of arable land of Asia was irrigated in 1994. Among Asian countries, India has the largest arable land, which is close to 39% of Asia's arable land. Only United States of America (USA) has more arable land than India.

The above data is extracted from an article of Shri Y.K. Alag, former Union Minister.

Fully understanding the history of a particular water dispute is also crucial for each side in the struggle. To wish away the history, to ignore the long-held perceptions of injustice or deprivation of any of the parties to the dispute, accomplishes but little. No current dispute in India started with a clean slate. The Narmada dispute began nearly forty years ago, the Cauvery dispute over a hundred years. Impatience with the past is inevitable, but forgetting it while indulging in shouting matches only polarises opinions further and drives down grudges more deeply.

The number and geographical configuration of the disputant states, the history of their interaction, and the social, economic and environmental stakes involved and the politics of each conflict have their special features. The dynamics of each conflict, and its national, state and local reverberations also differ from case to case. The end result for India is that its water politics is a highly-diverse and continually-changing challenge. Meeting the challenge will require strong institutions, a will to cooperate and a determination to be just.

Inequitable access to commons such as water is hardly surprising, given that it is a function of our stratified public realm where a tiny minority of elite corners most of the resources. What has, however, made matters worse is the emergence of a natural resource-intensive industry and modern water-intensive agriculture, with marginal social groups having virtually no say in the matter.

The National Water Policy which has assigned the highest priority for drinking water supply needs to be followed by irrigation, hydro-power, navigation and industrial, and other uses. In the successive FYPs and the intervening annual plans, efforts have been made to rapidly develop water supply and sanitation systems. In the context of the 'International Drinking Water Supply and Sanitation Decade', the (GOI) launched the decade programmes in April 1981 with a view to achieving population coverage of 100% water supply facilities in urban and rural areas, 80% sanitation facilities in urban areas and 25% sanitation facilities in rural areas, respectively, by the end of the decade, i.e. March 1991. However, due to financial and other constraints the targets originally set for the decade were scaled down to 90% in the case of urban water supply and 85% in the case of rural water supply, 50% in the case of urban sanitation and 5% in the case of rural sanitation, respectively. As per policy adopted provision for drinking water is to be made in all water resources projects. The drinking water requirements of most of the mega cities/cities in India are met from reservoirs of irrigation/multi-purpose schemes existing in nearby areas and even by long distance transfer. Delhi getting drinking water from Tehri Dam and Chennai city from Krishna Water through Telugu Ganga Project are typical example. Even for availing drinking water from inter-state rivers, there are disputes.

Advocating that politicians must assume the responsibility for making major decisions about water resource development does not absolve Central and state institutions from playing their respective roles in the process.

Whatever role the Centre and/or states might play in resolving the water disputes or whatever degree of responsibility politicians might assume for water resource development, disputes will continue to remain. This is due to the simple reason that the present strategies for the utilisation of our limited resources of country's water are not adequate to provide water to all for all purposes. A major departure in water utilisation strategies as well as acceleration of the speed with which water will be utilised is called for.

It is precisely with this strategy for changing the speed of development of our water resources and its economic use, that this book has been presented for the serious consideration of all stake holders who matter in the expeditious implementation of the proposals given therein; to ease the water problems of the country. The change in the strategy proposed is to utilise economically the available water by the universal use of the devices of sprinkler and drip systems to cultivate all crops in the country. A whole chapter in this book has been devoted to the methodology of this change for surface water as well as groundwater utilisation. At a very conservative estimate, this change will bring about 50% increase in utilisation of irrigated area, compared with the present conventional method of flood irrigation. The energy required to manage this distribution system can be met from non-conventional sources. It is also estimated that 50% of our cattle strength is enough for providing power required to run this system through biogas alone! Needless to mention, there are other sources available for generating non-conventional energy sources which are also mentioned in this study.

It is the objective spelt out in this book that by the year 2020 we have to utilise the country's ultimate irrigation potential of 140 million hectares, which by adoption of this changed methodology of utilisation will increase to 210 million hectares (50% rise). That is, area sown more than once will significantly rise.

As we may see from the book, this steep increase of irrigation potential will produce 478 million tonnes of foodgrains by the year 2020 itself while our requirement will be 376 million tonnes in that year, i.e. we will be left with a surplus of 102 million tonnes. Needless to mention that there will be very significant increase in the production of all other agricultural commodities also. So much so, a revolutionary change in the agricultural sector will be brought about. This book also presents a water budget which indicates how India will meet all its requirements for all sectors in the future.

The changed methodology will bring about a revolution in the secondary and tertiary sectors also. Industries to manufacture drip/sprinklers/pipes/ biogas plants and agricultural processing units will be forced to establish their units in the rural and peri-urban areas. This will be coupled with requirement of a huge force of para-technical personnel to carry out repairs and services of these installations. With marginal training of the rural youth this force can emerge and secure better incomes. In fact, recommendations have been made in brief and rural prosperity not hitherto seen will be brought about.

I am happy to present *Unleashing India – Water: Elixir of Life*.

Introduction

The National Water Policy for the twenty-first century has to recognise water as a national resource for the purpose of national development goals and planning, although the management of water has to be done in a decentralised way in partnership between local communities and the concerned state governments, adopting strategies which will economise use of water.

To minimise the negative impacts of the overuse and misuse of water and to ensure that our precious water resources are used optimally in removing poverty and achieving economic and human development, it is necessary that we have a water policy which recognises and adequately addresses the challenges we face and are going to face in the twenty-first century.

Some Manifestations of this Crisis

- There is hardly any city which receives 24-hour supply of drinking water.
- Many rural habitations which had been covered under the drinking water programme are now being reported as having slipped back with target dates for completion continuously pushed back. There are pockets where arsenic, nitrate, and fluoride in drinking water are posing a serious health hazard.
- In many parts, the groundwater table declines due to over-exploitation imposing an increasing financial burden on farmers who need to deepen their wells and replace their pump sets and on state governments whose subsidy burden for electricity supply rises.

- Many major and medium irrigation (MMI) projects seem to remain under execution forever as they slip from one plan to the other with enormous cost and time overruns.
- Owing to lack of maintenance, the capacity of the older systems seems to be going down.
- The gross irrigated area does not seem to be rising in a manner that it should be, given the investment in irrigation. The difference between potential created and area actually irrigated remains large. Unless we bridge the gap, significant increase in agricultural production will be difficult to realise.
- Floods are a recurring problem in many parts of the country. Degradation of catchment areas and loss of flood plains to urban development and agriculture have accentuated the intensity of floods.
- Water quality in our rivers and lakes is far from satisfactory. Water in most parts of rivers is not fit for bathing, let alone drinking. Untreated or partially treated sewage from towns and cities is being dumped into the rivers.
- Untreated or inadequately treated industrial effluents pollute water bodies and also contaminate groundwater.
- At the same time water conflicts are increasing. Apart from the traditional conflicts about water rights between upper and lower riparians in a river, conflicts about quality of water, people's right for rainwater harvesting in a watershed against downstream users, industrial use of groundwater and its impact on water tables and between urban and rural users have emerged.

The optimum utilisation of our water, land and natural resources is extremely important in achieving these objectives. Towards this end watershed management is an important input. This results in greater vegetative cover, *in-situ* conservation of soil, water and moisture. It also prevents inflow of silt into our reservoirs, tanks, rivers, etc. Thereby, our soil and water resources are conserved in a scientific manner. A detailed description of watershed management has been given in this book.

Besides taking care of urban and rural needs, maintaining the life of river systems and other water bodies should be an important objective of planning. Water quality has to be a very important aspect of water policy. The best way to ensure water quality is the prevention of pollution of water bodies and introduction of the 'polluter pays principle'. In addition, improvements in existing strategies and innovation of new techniques resting on a strong science and technology base will be needed to eliminate the pollution of surface and groundwater resources, to improve water quality and to step up the recycling and re-use of water.

Many rivers and underground aquifers often cut across state boundaries. Water as a resource is one and indivisible, as such rainfall, river waters, surface ponds, and lakes and groundwater are all part of one system; water is a part of a larger ecological system. Development of groundwater must take India's great hydro-geological diversity into account. Great caution needs to be exercised especially in hard rock regions that constitute a major part of India's land area. There should be a reassessment every ten years on a scientific basis of all forms of water, taking into consideration the quality of the water available for various uses.

Domestic Sector

- Introduction of domestic water saving devices
- Water metres on all consumers/groups of consumers
- Progressive water tariff structure
- Auditing of water balance on each distribution system
- Sewage and other domestic use to be piped out separately.

Industrial Sector

- Progressive water tariff
- Water recycling facilities
- Treated urban sewage water for cooling and other processes.

Agriculture Sector

- Water rates on volumetric basis to Water Users' Associations (WUAs) should be pegged at an appropriate level to yield enough revenue for maintenance costs

- Treated sewage water for non-edible crops
- Saline water for tolerant crops
- Improvement in irrigation practices and reduction of water losses
- Pressure irrigation systems to be introduced.

Coordinated development of surfacewater and groundwater and their conjunctive use should be envisaged right from the project planning stage and should form an essential part of the project. Over-exploitation of groundwater should be avoided near the coast to prevent ingress of sea water into sweet water aquifers.

The management of the water resources for diverse uses should be done by adopting a participatory approach: by involving not only the various governmental agencies but also the users and other stakeholders in an effective and decisive way in various aspects of planning, design, development and management of the water resources schemes.

All projects that seek to conserve/impound water or generate power should make the Environmental Impact Assessment (EIA), the Social Impact Assessment (SIA) and Cost Benefit Analysis open for public scrutiny and should examine alternate options before coming to a conclusion about the most appropriate strategy.

There should be water zoning of the country and the economic activities should be guided and regulated in accordance with such zoning. In planning operation systems, water allocation priorities should broadly be as below, but governed on the basis of local conditions and requirements.

1. Drinking and domestic use
2. Sustaining livelihoods
3. Sustaining environment, maintaining river systems and aquatic life
4. Irrigation and hydro-power
5. Thermal power and industries
6. Recreation and religious uses
7. Navigation.

The standard with regard to water allocated per capita for domestic use should be 30 to 60 litres per day. It may vary according to rainfall zones, i.e. less in Rajasthan and more in Assam, but should be the same for rural and urban areas. Sanitation requirement, however, should be considered separately.

A minimum good quality water flow should be ensured at all times as required for the life of the river and for sustaining livelihoods. This should include the allocation of water for various purposes including conserving the environment, preventing groundwater salinity and sea water intrusion, supporting livelihood based on aquatic life and other uses of water, recreation, and cultural activities like bathing and festivities. The requirement of water for these various purposes should be calculated scientifically. To begin with at least 50% of the lean period flow before the structure was built (average of 1-2 months) over and above the committed use should be allowed to go downstream of all existing and new structures.

In project planning, implementation and operation, the preservation of the quality of the environment and the ecological balance should be a primary consideration. Details of all effluents generated by each industry or urban area should be available to the public. Necessary legislation should be made for the preservation of the existing water bodies by preventing encroachment and deterioration of water quality. An annual list of defaulters in this regard with the extent of area under encroachment will be prepared and published by the pollution control board so that social and legal pressure can be brought to bear on the defaulters.

Traditional and natural wetlands and water bodies like tanks, *jheels, chors,* village ponds, etc., have been badly neglected in the last few decades. These structures should be restored, maintained and used properly and these water bodies should not be allowed to be encroached upon for any other land use.

Watershed management and minor irrigation projects would be most suitable for drought prone, tribal and hill areas, which should be allowed and encouraged to be developed by the local communities, with technical and financial help from the government and Non-Govermental Organisations (NGOs).

Irrigation and Hydropower

Irrigation planning either in an individual project or in a basin, as a whole should take into account the irrigability of land, cost effective irrigation options possible from all available sources (including traditional ones). Irrigation efficiency in irrigation projects should be improved from the present average of 35% to the maximum achievable, which is approximately 60%.

Water allocation in an irrigation system should be done with due regard to equity and social justice. Disparities in the availability of water between head-reach and tail-end farms, and between large and small farms will be obviated by adoption of the changed methodology of distribution of water use through micro-hydel devices of sprinkler/drip which have been recommended in this book for universal use. Further, another recommendation covers that all alkaline and saline land should be reclaimed before introducing micro-hydel system of distribution. Once this system is introduced due to economic use of water, alkalinity and salinity will disappear or will appear in micro-extents which can be instantly cured.

The prioritisation of projects basin-wise and state-wise is needed. Due to the extreme paucity of funds, projects should be prioritised in such a way that those on-going projects where over 20% of the project cost has already been incurred should be completed first.

So far the utilisation of potential created on an irrigation project is one of the main criteria for its performance. Often, there is an over-estimate of potential, so as to indicate a better B/C ratio and Rate of Return.

In certain projects, it may be power generation, drinking water or flood control, which may be the major component, rather than irrigation. Thus, instead of being based on the area irrigated or height of the dam, projects should now be categorised on the basis of live storage capacity. Projects above 100 MCM would be categorised as major, between 10 and 100 MCM would be medium; and those below 10 MCM would be minor. Projects smaller than 1 MCM would be categorised as micro. For run of the river schemes, the volume of water diverted in a year would determine the categorisation of the project as major, medium, minor or micro.

The first right to groundwater should be to the concerned community and not to an individual on land-ownership basis. In areas with scarcity of water, the respective community organisations should have the right to inspect and monitor the use of groundwater by private landowners to ensure that groundwater beyond permissible limits is not being withdrawn. The detrimental environmental consequences of over-exploitation of groundwater need to be effectively prevented by legislation and its enforcement by local government bodies, RWAs and gram sabhas, who will have to play a vital role in this. To give teeth to their actions the Central and state governments should enact suitable legislation and notify the permissible water depths to which groundwater depletion will be permitted for each region/block/gram sabha/ watershed after identifying the special problems of each area.

Flood Management and Drainage

Insurance against floods and droughts requires local action as well as national coordination. It is essential to realise that floods and their negative consequences can only be managed, they cannot be 'controlled'.

A number of systematic measures that include the adoption of suitable policies, operational and managerial steps, disaster preparedness, flood forecasting, ecological measures and international river water sharing agreements should be taken urgently to deal with floods in such a way that their intensity is moderated and the negative consequences on flood-prone populations are minimised. The planning for flood management should be done in a holistic manner so that the needs during the non-flood season are also taken care of.

There should be a master plan for flood control and management for each flood-prone basin. An integrated river basin water policy for states sharing a river basin should be evolved.

In those instances where flood control is one of the key purposes of multi-purpose dams, it should be ensured that the dam intercepts significantly at least 33% of the catchment/drainage above the affected area. Wherever dams and reservoirs exist or contemplated for multi-purpose benefits, flood management should be integrated among its purposes. In highly flood prone areas, flood management should be given overriding consideration in reservoir regulation policy even at the cost of sacrificing some irrigation or power benefits.

While physical flood protection works like embankments and dykes may be necessary in some areas, increased emphasis should be laid on non-physical measures such as flood forecasting and warning, flood-plain zoning and flood proofing, for the minimisation of losses, so as to reduce the recurring expenditure on flood relief.

Land-use regulation should be integrated with flood plain zoning to avoid inappropriate landuse in flood-plains and other flood-prone areas and consequent higher damages and relief costs in the long run. Flood-prone areas should be demarcated at different probability levels and appropriate development measures and economic activities should be devised for flood- prone and non-flood-prone areas. Unauthorised and unabated encroachment in the flood plains and riverbeds as also cultivation of riverbeds/drainage courses during the flood period should be prevented.

Watershed management through extensive soil conservation measures, such as check dams, contour trenches, etc., preservation of forests, increasing the forest cover, etc. should be promoted to reduce the intensity of floods. The traditional flood management systems of the area should be revitalised, maintained and suitably upgraded. The traditional method of building houses on stilts, for instance, should be revived and encouraged. Thus, the government policy should build on people's resolve to live with floods and should aim at dealing with floods so as to minimise losses and hardship while obtaining certain benefits. Construction of embankments should be considered only after careful detailed studies and investigations as a part of a package.

Drainage

Draining out of water becomes necessary for the following purposes:

- To get rid of bad quality water from sewage and industrially used water; this can be avoided by treating the water and re-using it.
- To recover land waterlogged and affected with salinity and alkalinity, it has to be reclaimed one time before introducing the proposed micro-hydel system of distribution envisaged in this book. This will mitigate this problem which should be attended instantly if it appears in micro form because inflow of water to plants will be by pipes with sprinklers/drips and the outflow of water through drainage channels.
- Wetland and other water bodies both natural and man-made should be used, without reclaiming it for landuse without water. These can be used for aquaculture, recharge of groundwater, maintaining ecology as in mangrove or rain forests, etc.

- To get rid of excess water during monsoon season due to sudden heavy rainfall. If natural depression, wetlands, tanks, can be properly maintained and even more created to absorb water and retain it during wet season and land with water, used for various economic purpose. This way, flood intensity could be moderated and water does not flow to the sea unused.

Land for land in respect of agriculturists should be the preferred option in those regions and states where land for resettlement is or can be made available. In some cases, where allotting land for land is not possible due to small holdings throughout the command, following alternative measures should be taken:

- Annuity for a certain number of years, where the amount of annuity and the number of years for which it is to be paid may be worked out on the basis of factors like skill level, value of loss of livelihood, and number of remaining years of active working life.
- A suitable job in the development project itself, where the skill and job profile match or person's skill can be upgraded by suitable training and only where the job is expected to be of a permanent nature, and is not merely created for the purpose of rehabilitation.

All water and power development projects should ensure that benefits of the project go to the local people first. For example, water supply and electric connections should be provided on priority to all local people who are affected.

The concerned government should appoint an independent agency (outside the project implementation) to monitor the R&D activities at regular intervals for the whole duration of the development project.

There are several land-based programmes being serviced by different ministries of the GOI. The important land-based programmes are: Drought Prone Area Programme (DPAP), Desert Development Programme (DDP), National Watershed Development Project for Rainfed Areas (NWDPRA), Integrated Watershed Development Programme (IWDP), and soil conservation in the catchments of river valley projects and flood-prone rivers.

Legal Changes

a) Setting up of river boards, both within states and inter-state, to plan in an integrated way for the development of water resources within a river basin. The necessary legislation should provide for the two-tier constitution of river boards, consisting of the river basin assembly and a supporting technical body. River basin organisations within states can be set up by Government Orders under existing legislation itself.

b) Enabling full and effective participation of the farmers and rural and urban communities in the task of managing water resources. The existing legislative framework, which provides overriding control over water resources to the state, should be modified to provide usufruct rights to local communities and a pivotal role in the management of water resources at the local level.

c) Regulation of groundwater so as to prevent and stop the overuse and depletion of groundwater in many areas. The existing law provides for control and ownership of groundwater by the landowner. This should be modified by transferring at least the management of groundwater to the gram sabha and the RWA. The overuse of groundwater should be stopped and regulated by the respective gram sabhas/RWAs, with higher levels of government providing the necessary information, framing rules for regulation and monitoring the situation.

d) Provision of accurate and up-to-date information on water resources in the public domain in a user-friendly form. This is essential for the rational and integrated planning of water resources in the country, for involving local communities in the task of management of water resources and for smooth resolution of water related conflicts between different parties. The Official Secrets Act and the attitudes and practices relating to its interpretation should be modified in order that information on water resources in the country is freely available.

There should be a system to monitor the performance of the project and socio-economic impact of the project. Such a monitoring process should take the community into confidence by involving them at every stage.

There is an urgent need for a paradigm shift in the management of water resources sector. From the present emphasis on the creation and expansion of water resources infrastructure for diverse uses, there is now a need to give greater emphasis to performance improvement of the existing water resource facilities.

There should be proper organisational arrangements at the national and state levels for ensuring the safety of storage dams and other water-related structures consisting of specialists in investigation, design, construction, hydrology, geology, etc. Dam safety legislation should be enacted to ensure proper inspection, maintenance and surveillance of the existing dams and also to ensure proper planning, investigation, design, construction and safety of new dams. The guidelines on the subject should be kept under constant review and periodically updated and reformulated. There should be a system of continuous surveillance and regular visits by experts.

The environmental and rehabilitation aspects have not been up to the mark, particularly in terms of implementation in the existing projects and those under construction.

A target of providing water to everybody within next five years, particularly in all the rural areas and especially where the quality of water is not up to the mark, should be fixed. However, after this, certain areas would still come up where the quality has deteriorated and as such would have to be given a new source of supply or better treatment of the water available.

Treatment of water from industries and sewage should be implemented within the next ten years.

Far too many projects are under construction at the present moment and it would be necessary to provide funds on priority for those on which more than 20% of expenditure or physical progress has been made for completion in the next five to ten years with practically no new projects to be taken up during these years. Some of the existing projects would need to be modernised, which should be the next priority and completed within the next ten years. The third priority should be to complete all hydro and irrigation projects within each basin by the year 2020.

Water is a prime natural resource, a basic human need and a precious national asset. Planning, development and management of water resources need to be governed by national perspective.

Floods and droughts affect vast areas of the country, transcending state boundaries. One-sixth area of the country is drought-prone. Out of 40 million hectare of the flood-prone area in the country, on an average, floods affect an area of around 7.5 million hectare per year. Approach to management of droughts and floods has to be coordinated and guided at the national level.

Growth process and the expansion of economic activities inevitably lead to increasing demands for water for diverse purposes: domestic including livestock, industrial, agricultural, hydro-power, thermal-power, navigation, recreation, etc.

Water Allocation Priorities

In the planning and operation of systems, water allocation priorities should be broadly as follows:

- Drinking water
- Irrigation
- Hydro-power
- Ecology
- Agro-industries and non–agricultural industries
- Navigation and other uses.

However, the priorities could be modified or added if warranted by the area/region specific considerations.

Irrigation

Irrigation planning either in an individual project or in a basin as a whole should take into account the irrigability of land, cost-effective irrigation options possible from all available sources of water and appropriate irrigation techniques for optimising water use efficiency.

There should be a close integration of water-use and land-use policies. Water allocation in an irrigation system should be done with due regard to equity and social justice. Disparities in the availability of water between head-reach and tail-end farms, and between large and small farms will be obviated by adoption of a new strategy of distribution of water through micro-hydel devices.

Concerted efforts should be made to ensure that the irrigation potential created is fully utilised. For this purpose, the command area development approach should be adopted in all irrigation projects.

Irrigation being the largest consumer of fresh water, the aim should be to get optimal productivity per unit of water. Scientific water management, farm practices and sprinkler and drip system of irrigation should be adopted in a universal manner using the methodology indicated in this book.

Management of the water resources for diverse uses should incorporate a participatory approach; by involving not only the various governmental agencies but also the users and other stakeholders, in an effective and decisive manner, in various aspects of planning, design, development and management of the water resources schemes. Necessary legal and institutional changes should be made at various levels for the purpose, duly ensuring appropriate role for women. Water Users' Association (WUAs) and the local bodies such as municipalities and gram panchayats should particularly be involved in the operation, maintenance and management of water infrastructures/facilities at appropriate levels progressively, with a view to eventually transfer the management of such facilities to the user groups/local bodies.

Science and Technology

For effective and economical management of our water resources, the frontiers of knowledge need to be pushed forward in several directions by intensifying research efforts in various areas, including the following:

- Hydrometeorology;
- Snow and lake hydrology;
- Surface and groundwater hydrology;
- River morphology and hydraulics;
- Assessment of water resources;
- Water harvesting and groundwater recharge;
- Water quality;
- Water conservation;
- Evaporation and seepage losses;
- Re-cycling and re-use;

- Better water management practices and improvements in operational technology;
- Crops and cropping systems;
- Soils and material research;
- New construction materials and technology (with particular reference to roller compacted concrete, fiber reinforced concrete, new methodologies in tunnelling technologies instrumentation, advanced numerical analysis in structures and back analysis);
- Seismology and seismic design of structures;
- The safety and longevity of water-related structures
- Economical designs for water resources projects;
- Risk analysis and disaster management;
- Use of remote sensing techniques in development and management;
- Use of static groundwater resource as a crisis management measure;
- Sedimentation of reservoirs;
- Use of sea water resources
- Prevention of salinity ingress
- Prevention of waterlogging and soil salinity
- Reclamation of waterlogged and saline lands
- Environmental impact
- Regional equity
- Computerised control of micro-hydel devices of sprinkler/drip services should be adopted in such a way that water is supplied to plants only when it is necessary and in optimal quantity required.

It is generally observed that the Tribunals set up for resolving inter-State issues take considerable time to give decision/awards. The matter received attention of Sarkaria Commission. The Sarkaria Commission in its report at Chapter XVII on Inter-State River Water Disputes has recommended that:

- Once an application under Section 3 of the Inter-State River Water Disputes Act (33 of 1956) is received from a State, it should be mandatory on the Union Government to constitute a Tribunal within a period not exceeding one year from the date of receipt of the application of any disputant State. The Inter-State River Water Disputes Act may be suitably amended for this purpose.

- The Inter-State Water Disputes Act should be amended to empower the Union Government to appoint a Tribunal, *suo-moto*, if necessary, when it is satisfied that such a dispute exists in fact.
- There should be a Data Bank and information system at the national level and adequate machinery should be set up for this purpose at the earliest. There should also be a provision in the Inter-State Water Disputes Act that states shall be required to give necessary data for which purpose the Tribunal may be vested with powers of a court.
- The Inter-State Water Disputes Act should be amended to ensure that the award of a Tribunal becomes effective within five years from the date of constitution of a Tribunal. If, however, for some reasons, a Tribunal feels that the five years period has to be extended, the Union Government may on a reference made by the Tribunal extend its term.
- The Inter-State Water Disputes Act, 1956 should be amended so that a Tribunal's award has the same force and sanction behind it as an order or decree of the Supreme Court to make a Tribunal's award really binding.

The recommendation of the Standing Committee on this item is as below:

> The Tribunal should give its award within a period of three years from the date of its constitution. However, if for unavoidable reasons the award could not be given within a period of three years, the Union Government may extend the period suitably not exceeding two years. The award should be implemented within two years from the date of notification of the award. If for unavoidable reasons the award could not be implemented within a period of two years the Union Government may extend the period suitably.

The above recommendation of its implementation will not resolve the problems confronting the country. Comprehensive, precise, faster and inclusive approach is the need of the hour.

World oceans cover about three-fourths of earth's surface. According to the UN estimates, the total amount of water on earth is about 1,400 million cubic kilometre which is enough to cover the earth with a layer of 3,000 metres depth. However, the fresh water constitutes a very small proportion of this enormous quantity. About 2.7% of the total water available on the earth is fresh water of which about 75.2% lies frozen in Polar regions and another 22.6% is present as groundwater. The rest is available in lakes, rivers, atmosphere, moisture, soil and vegetation. What is effectively available for consumption and other uses is a small proportion of the quantity available in rivers, lakes and groundwater. The crisis about water resources development and management thus arises because most of the water is not available for use, and second, it is characterised by its highly uneven spatial distribution. Accordingly, the importance of water has been recognised and greater emphasis is being laid on its economic use and better management.

Water on the earth is in motion through the hydrological cycle. The utilisation of water for most of the users, i.e. human, animal or plant involve movement of water. The dynamic and renewable nature of the water resources and the recurrent need for its utilisation requires that water resources are measured in terms of its flow rates. Thus, water resources have two facets. The dynamic resource, measured as flow is more relevant for most of developmental needs. The static or fixed nature of the reserve, involving the quantity of water, the length of area of the water bodies is also relevant for some activities like pisciculture, navigation, etc.

Conclusion

In view of the vital importance of water for human and animal life, for maintaining ecological balance, and for economic and development activities of all kinds, and considering its increasing scarcity, the planning and management of this resource and its optimal, economical and equitable use has become a matter of utmost urgency. Concerns of the community needs is to be taken into account for water resources development and management. The success of the National Water Policy will depend entirely on evolving and maintaining a national consensus and commitment to its underlying principles and objectives. To achieve the desired objectives, State

Water Policy backed with an operational action plan shall be formulated in a time-bound manner, say, in two years. National Water Policy may be revised periodically as and when need arises.

1

Historical Background

A perusal of the world history indicates the close link between irrigation and civilisations. Great civilisations across the world have sprung even in the millenniums before Christ in valleys of the Nile, the Indus, the Euphrates and the Tigris, because water was used for irrigation.

In '3000 BC, King Menes, dammed the Nile and diverted its course. Among the most interesting artifacts remaining, is the Sadd El Kafra (Dam of pagans) built in 2800 BC, just south of Cairo. It was apparently built without a spillway and with a capacity, so small in relation to its catchment area that it failed early in its lifetime'.[1] The Egyptians were more successful in distributing the flood water than collecting it. In the plains of the Nile which were flooded each year during the monsoon seasons of July-September, they sub-divided such plains into plots of lands with embankments so that flood water may be stored and later used. In addition' diversion of Nile into huge flood storage scheme (Lake Moeris), which was excavated according to Herodotus in the 19th Century BC'[2] was another facility for storing water. However, others have considered it as a natural feature and not an excavated work.

---

[1]Malcom, Newson; *Land, Water and Development: Sustainable Management of River Basin Systems* (Second Edition); London and New York: Routledge, p. 3
[2]Ibid. p.3

'Emperor Yu in China began to control rivers in the interest of land reclamation. As Biswas (1967, p.120) recorded "he studied the rivers . . . he mastered the water"; it is clear from the Chinese literature that mapping of river networks and consequently, some concept of river basin had been born.'[3]

In Sumerian and Babylonian case, where irrigation system of Euphrates and Tigris worked smoothly, it was the centralised control of the government that made it function so. In fact, this control was even codified by King Hammurabi 'the code of Hammurabi (1750) is a codification of Sumerian and Babylonian water law. Flood damage due to negligence was particularly feared.'[4] Under these laws, there appear to have been farmer(s) responsible for keeping the dam intact. If there was any breach in the dam and other farmers' fields were flooded, the lands of such responsible farmers were being sold to replace the corn of others which was destroyed. The same applied to the distribution system; if any farmer opened the inlet or outlet of the field in a manner careless enough to allow water to overflow and flood neighbouring lands, he was also liable to pay to such neighbouring farmers prescribed fine. All this type of control lasted so long as this region was under a strong single Central Government, but in course of time, 'Sumerian society became partitioned into a number of local city states'[5] which led to its collapse.

'Another prehistoric achievement in the Middle East was the building of quanats, underground drainage channels conveying waters from springs to consumers (in some cases more than 30 km distance was covered), at a constant gradient free from pollution or losses from evaporation.'[6] Groundwater exploitation and underground storage of water are also noted in both Egypt and Mesopotamia. Clearly, therefore, potable water supplies to urban centres were also a feature of hydrologic civilisations.

2750 BC sees the origin of the Indus valley water supply and drainage systems. Even in the Indus valley archaeological records indicate that water supplies were made to houses and drainage systems have been found dating

---

[3]Ibid. p.5

[4]Ibid. p.5

[5]Ibid. p.2-3

[6]Ibid. p.5

from 2200 BC. That, Mohanjadaro and Harrappa practised agriculture as main occupation is amply evident by the existence of food products like rice, wheat, barley, peas, sesame, etc. The cultivation of such foodstuffs depends on good supply of water and hence, efficient water supply arrangement must have been there. Indus valley civilisation claims Raikes 'it could have survived and prospered on zero rainfall with or without irrigation for, the Indus complex of rivers enjoys a well-marked seasonal flood that would have inundated vast areas of flood plain (p. 113). Even with today's barrages and levees, he claims, uncontrollable flooding still occurs'[7]. Toyanbee stresses the magnitude and scale of Indus civilisation, with its two principal cities, 400 miles apart he does not consider the management problems of such a scale: possibly management failed to respond in a coordinated way, to the environmental change, however caused. However uniquely, it seems the Indus valley civilisation ended as a result of profound environmental change of climate, causing damaging floods and prolonged droughts, which overcame the sophistication of the engineering (existing then). Indus valley civilisation might have perished due to whatever reason, but the 5,000 years old knowledge of our tradition, has continued in various parts of India to harness water for human betterment.

In Appendix 1, alongwith Kautilya's views a couple of India's historical marvels in irrigation, long before the coming into being of the British Raj (including a part of the Raj's contribution), have been explained in detail. India had evolved its own systems, ideally suited to its genius and environment. The one factor which runs commonly throughout its history; whether in north or south, east or west, is that, although the rulers or philanthropists or temples or people themselves created the irrigation systems or works, either with State help or on their own, but in their maintenance the people everywhere played, an active role. The concept of *kudimaramath* (self-repair) of irrigation and drainage works was evolved by the Vijayanagara kings. Kudimaramath, by local custom was performed by the joint labour of the village community. Usually, the farmers possessing lands near sources of water supply provided labour required for the works at a fixed rate for deepening river beds or removing silt from other water sources, thereby giving rise to the system of Kudimaramath. The

[7]Ibid. p.6

Vijayanagar kings kept such contributions in view and did not collect cess, from land owners on a uniform basis to meet the cost of Kudimaramath. The Vijaynagar Empire's agricultural policies were based primarily on expansion of irrigation network and its appropriate maintenance; which led to collection of increased revenues to the state. Despite this, the state was giving concession in cesses wherever people involved themselves in the programme of Kudimaramath, in order to give a feeling that, they are not merely taxed but also their contribution was recognised by the state to deserve this compensation in the shape of waiver of cesses. It should be recognised that, this was a very sensible policy parameter for an economy, which was primarily agrarian.

British Rule

With the advent of the British, the major predetermining factor for the promulgation of the policies of the state was collection of revenues from land, whether irrigated or unirrigated. 'The state became the "universal landlord" and land revenue became its primary objective.'[8] And, the state became the owners of the water sources also. In Madras province, in the last decades of the eighteenth century and the early nineteenth century, various forms of land revenue administration, were experimented by trial and error, resulting in instability of land tenure and cultivation, and neglect of irrigation works because peoples' involvement was reduced to almost zero. Finally, Raiyatwari settlement was introduced. 'In 1855, a quarter of century after the principle of Raiyatwari were introduced it was found that less than 1/5th of the area of the Madras province was cultivated, while more than half the area recorded arable, remained waste'.[9] Under the Raiyatwari settlement, the responsibility for commonly owned properties like tanks vested with government and therefore, the maintenance responsibilities devolved on revenue officials who were not equipped for the task. Civil engineers of the army were then given the power to take care of irrigation

---

[8]*State of India's Environment 4 – A Citizen Report, Dying Wisdom – Rise, Fall and Potential of India's Traditional Water Harvesting Systems* by Centre for Science and Environment, p. 300.
[9]Ibid. p. 300

works. 'Then an office of the Superintendent of Tank Repairs was created in 1809 and a separate department of tanks in 1819 which was precursor of Public Works Department (PWD). PWD itself was formed in 1858 in Tamil Nadu (erstwhile Madras province) and 1855-56 in Mysore'.[10] Thus, for the first time in the history of irrigation, 'a modern centralised system was put in place whose primary interest was collection of land revenue and which, therefore, brought both land and water under centralised control'.[11] This is reflected by their administration in Bombay province also. The nationalist economic historian Romesh Chandra Dutt states 'The dominions of the last Maratha Peshwa passed under British rule in 1817 and that land revenue was continuously raised from that year. From 1817, revenue realised from the newly acquired territory was Rs 80 lakh, in 1818 it was raised to Rs 115 lakh and a few more years later it was Rs 150 lakhs per annum'.[12] The village community system broke down under pressure and the Raiyatwari system was introduced by Sir Thomas Monroe in Madras and a similar Raiyatwari system was adopted in Bombay; i.e. a system of separate settlements of individual cultivators. Even with this set-up which was based on revenue and increased revenue, both on irrigated and unirrigated land, the British government tried to enforce compulsorily system for repair or irrigation works. The Vijayanagar kings used to give due considerations to the *cultivators*, who contributed labour for this system while collecting cess. In other words, the labour fees were remitted by the government of Vijayanagara kings in the tax. On the other hand, British relied on Madras Compulsory Labour Act 1858 to make lawful the enforcement of compulsory labour, whenever breaches occurred due to inundations. But obviously, the government failed to secure cooperation from the people. All that the British did was to confer legal power to declare government ownership of land and water, and assume the power to tax. In their desire to rule and exploit, they destroyed the water management systems built and maintained by the rural communities of India over centuries.

Similarly, in Bengal the vibrant flood irrigation system run by parallel canals taken out from several rivers in the deltas of the Ganga and Damodar

---

[10]Ibid. p. 301

[11]Ibid. p. 301

[12]Ibid. p. 301

was given up, and was rendered non-functional, purely due to the inability of the administration to appreciate that the parallel canals from all the major and minor rivers supplied water with fertile silt and fish, and fish carp were abundantly available everywhere. This was resulting in not only high production due to improved fertility of soil resulting from securing of fresh silt coupled with availability of abundant water and fish or fish carp which were eating malaria larvae. The British being traders and navigators started embanking the major rivers and thereby blocking canals, which resulted in a rich and fertile province with a healthy population being charged to a famine struck, disease-prone land with agricultural production, drastically coming down' (vide Appendix 1 for details).

The wrong revenue policies of commutation of produce rent system to cash rent system in Bihar made the landlords relinquish their responsibilities for keeping the ahar pyne system intact in south Bihar (details in Appendix 1).

In other parts of India, also the government takeover had had its impact on indigenous systems of irrigation. At least one thing is undisputable which is that with absolute power in British hands over land and water, we appear to have given full power of attorney to the British PWD to maintain our irrigation works, so that we may relax and suffer for want of water. We have still not recovered from that suffering because we depend on the state to even maintain our minor irrigation works. So much so that the feeder channels have been silted up, the tank holding capacities have been reduced, the *bunds* and the weirs continue to be weak. The pre-British spirit of Kudhimaramat of the Vijayanagara Empire should have to be brought back by appropriate policy changes, both in execution and maintenance of irrigation works and in collection of water rates, part of which can be deployed for maintenance by the WUAs. Next the British took interest in the major irrigation works on rivers, since it offered great scope for centrally controlled management. Their achievements can be recorded as under.

In the nineteenth century, the western Yamuna canal which was built in the fourteenth century by the Mughals was renovated. Irrigation development, in the British period was financed by the revenue collected and efforts to promote irrigation, through private companies with government guarantee of 5% on capital invested was unsuccessful. In 1866, important changes were made in the principles and policies governing the execution and financing of irrigation projects. Keeping in view that large investment was required to expand irrigation and poor response to privatisation, it was decided that irrigation projects would be executed only by the states and would be financed from public loans. A number of projects like Sir Hind Canal (Punjab) lower Ganga Canal, Agra Canal, Betwa Canal (UP), Periyar System (Tamil Nadu), Mutha Canals (Maharashtra) were completed.

In 1901, GOI appointed the 'Indian Irrigation Commission' to report on irrigation as a protection against famine in India. Based on the Commission's recommendations, The Triple Canal Project now in Pakistan, Tribeni Canal (Bihar), Godavari Canal, Pravara Canal and Neera Right Bank Canal (Maharashtra), Sarda Canal (Uttar Pradesh) and Mahanadi Canal (Madhya Pradesh) were completed.

A significant change in the policy governing the administration and financing of irrigation projects was brought about with the introduction of Montague-Chelmsford Reforms in 1921. The provincial governments were authorised to raise loan themselves for financing of irrigation. Krishnaraja Sagar (Karnataka), Nizam Sagar (Andhra Pradesh), Mettur Dam (Tamil Nadu), Bikaner Canal (Rajasthan), Sutlej Valley Canals and Sukkur Barrage (now in Pakistan) were taken up by the provinces after this authorisation.

In 1935, the British Parliament passed the GOI Act 1935, according to which the subject of irrigation was transferred from the control of Centre to the provincial or state governments. The centre was no longer concerned with the development of irrigation except where disputes arose among co-basin states. The Constitution makers after Independence thought it prudent to continue this arrangement resulting in centre, totally losing all control over irrigation. Much of the malaise confronting irrigation today can be traced back to this decision of 1935.

Table 1 gives the development of irrigation in the pre-Independence period to the extent available.

Table 1
(in million Hectares)

Years	Cultivated area	Total irrigated area	% of irrigated area to cultivate area
1896-1900	Not available	11.98	–
1901-1905	72.71	13.15	18
1906-1910	78.09	15.95	20
1911-1915	82.79	18.01	22
1916-1920	84.08	18.42	22
1921-1925	82.55	18.62	23
1926-1930	84.77	18.94	22
1931-1935	85.02	18.94	22
1936-1940	85.82	22.06	26
1941-1945	87.24	22.60	26

(Source: Planning Commission, GOI)

COMMENTS

Cultivated Area

From 72.71 million hectares at the end of 1905, the cultivated area increased to 87.24 million hectares by the end of 1945; or, cultivated area increased by 14.53 million hectares from 1905 to 1945 or an increase of 20% in forty years, i.e. 0.5% per year.

Irrigated Area

In forty years from 1905 to 1945, the irrigated area increased from 13.15 million hectares to 22.60 million hectares or an increase of 9.45 million hectares or 72% of the area in the period from 1905 to 1945 in forty years. The increase was 1.8% per annum on an average. But if we consider 1900 figure of 11.98 million hectares, the area increased from 11.98 million hectares in 1900 to 22.6 million hectares in 1945 or in forty-five years the increase was 22.60 - 11.98 = 10.62 million hectares or in percentage terms, it had increased by 89% or an increase of 1.9% or 2% per annum during absolute British rule (1900-45). Prior to 1896, say, in the nineteenth century, what area in the country existed under irrigation was not available to us. Maybe, it was much more or equal, because we have seen that many indigenous systems were unwittingly destroyed by the ruler's policies.

2

Irrigation – Progress Post-1945

By 1945, the British stranglehold had weakened due to the Indian freedom struggle. They were involving Indians in district boards/ provincial governments. By 1946, even the Central Government came under the control of interim government headed by Indian ministers, although the Viceroy and Governors continued to be British. Needless to say, from 15 August 1947, the absolute power came in the hands of the Indians. Therefore, if we consider that from 1945 to date what has been done in the field of irrigation has been done by us, we will not be wrong. And, what has been done by us up to March end 2002 is given in Table 2:

Table 2
Ultimate irrigation potential, potential created and utilised

Up to March 2002 since inception *(Million Hectares)*

Sl No	Category	Potential created up to March 2002	Potential utilised up to March 2002	Utilisation as % of potential created
1	Major Medium	36.92	30.92	83
2	Minor	56.90	49.05	86
3	Total	93.82	79.97	85

(Tenth Five Year Plan – Mid-term appraisal, vide appendix No.2)

The following points emerge from Table 2:

1. From Table 1, we know that the irrigated area reported in 1945 was 22.60 million hectare and by 2002, we have seen from Table 2 that, the area under irrigation potential utilised has increased to 79.97 million hectares or an increase of 79.97-22.60 = 57.37 million hectares in fifty-seven years, or about a million hectares per annum has been the average annual achievement from 1945 to March 2002.
2. In percentage terms 57.37 million hectares increase or 254% over 1945 position of 22.60 million hectares. That is the average annual in fifty-seven years (from 1945 to 2002) increase was 4.5% per annum. That is, during absolute British rule in fifty years it was annual average increase of 2% per annum and with reigns of power for fifty-seven years in our hand it was an increase to 4.5% per annum.
3. Another point which emerges from Table 2 is that, we have by 2002 utilised 79.97 or 80 million hectares of irrigation potential as against our presently assessed ultimate irrigation potential of 139.90 or 140 million hectares. We have a gap of 140-80 = 60 million hectares. That is, the balance of potential yet to be utilised as at the end of March 2002 will be 60 million hectares. At the observed annual rate of 1 million hectares per annum from 1945 to 2002, we will take another sixty years from March 2002 to utilise our ultimate irrigation potential. In other words, we will utilise our ultimate irrigation potential of 140 million hectares by the end of March 2062, unless we take steps to hasten the process.
4. A further point which emerges from Table 2 is that, between creation of irrigation potential and its utilisation, there was a gap of 93.82–79.97 = 13.85 million hectares or 14 million hectares. A huge gap!

Tenth Five Year Plan Performance

If we consider Tenth Five Year Plan (FYP) (April 2002 to March 2007) targets and its performance, which is available for 2002-03 to 2004-05 in terms of targets and anticipated achievement, both for creation of irrigation potential and utilisation which is given in two tables we may be able to create and utilise irrigation potential a little earlier. The Tenth FYP targets and achievements of creation and utilisation are given in Table 3.

Table 3

Tenth Five Year Plan targets and achievements anticipated in creation of irrigation potential (April 2002 to March 2005)

(million hectares)

Sl No	Category of Irrigation	Tenth Five Year Plan target for creation of irrigation potential	2002-03		2003-04		Targets 2004-05	Total of anticipated achievements of three years from 2002 to 2005 ** (Columns 5+7+8)
			Target	Anticipated achievement	Target	Anticipated achievement		
1	2	3	4	5	6	7	8	9
1	Major – Medium	9.94	1.50	0.81 *	1.34	1.00	1.55	3.36
2	Minor Irrigation	6.81	0.82	0.69	0.71	0.70	0.75	2.14
	TOTAL	16.75	2.32	1.50	2.05	1.70	2.30	5.50

(Vide Appendix 2 for details)

*Actual achievement, ** includes targets 2004-05

Table 3A
Tenth Five Year Plan (April 2002 to March 2005)
Targets for utilisation of irrigation potential

(million hectares)

Sl No	Category of Irrigation	X Five FYP target for utilisation of irrigation potential	2002-2003		2003-2004		Targets 2004-5	Total of anticipated achievements of three years from 2002 to 2005 ** (incl. Target of 2004-05) Total of columns 5+7+8
			Target	Anticipated achievement	Target	Anticipated achievement		
1	2	3	4	5	6	7	8	9
1	Major–Medium	6.19	0.98	0.53*	0.89	0.66	1.02	2.21
2	Minor–Irrigation	5.44	0.66	0.55	0.57	0.56	0.60	1.71
	TOTAL	11.63	1.64	1.08	1.46	1.22	1.62	3.92

(Vide Appendix 2 for details)

*actual achievement, ** target 2004-05 included

Table 3B

Irrigation Potential Created and Potential Utilised since Inception till March 2005 end

(million hectares)

Sl No.	Category	Potential created			Potential utilized			Balance of potential created and yet to be utilised at the end of March-2005
		Up to end of March 2002 since inception	During April 2002 – March 2005	Total Cols. (3+4)	Up to end of March 2002 since inception	During April 2002 – March -2005	Total Cols. (6+7)	
1	2	3	4	5	6	7	8	9
1.	Major/ Medium Irrigation	36.92	3.36	40.28	30.92	2.21	33.13	7.15
2.	Minor Irrigation	56.90	2.14	59.04	49.05	1.71	50.76	8.28
	TOTAL	93.82	5.50	99.32	79.97	3.92	83.89	15.43

From Table 3 it is seen that, the anticipated achievement of progress of creation of irrigation potential up to end of March 2005 will be; potential created up to end of March 2002, i.e. 93.82 million hectares (vide Table 2)+5.50 million hectares anticipated achievement up to end of March 2005 = 99.32 million hectares since inception up to end of March 2005. From column 9 of Table 3, it can be seen that the creation of irrigation potential's annual average of first three years of Tenth FYP is 5.50/3 = 1.80 million hectares per annum. We also know that, our ultimate irrigation potential is 140 million hectares. Thus, the balance of irrigation potential to be created will be 140 million hectares – achievement up to end of March 2005 of 99.32 million hectares = 40.68 million hectares.

It is seen in Table 3A that the anticipated achievement of utilisation of irrigation potential created up to end of March 2005, will be 79.97 million hectares (achievement up to end of March 2002 as per Table 2)+3.92 million hectares (achievement anticipated up to end of March 2005) = 83.89 million hectares are anticipated to be achieved, since inception up to end of March 2005. From column 9 of Table 3A it can be seen that, the annual average utilisation of irrigation potential of the first three years of Tenth FYP will be 3.92/3 = 1.31 million hectares which is a slight improvement over the annual average achievement of the period 1945 to 2002, which we have seen as only 1 million hectares per hectare. In Table 3B below we have presented the potential created and potential utilised since inception, up to end of March 2005.

Note: From Table 3B the following inferences can be drawn:

i. Since, 78% of minor irrigation potential is utilised under groundwater sources (vide Appendix 3) the groundwater potential utilised up to March 2005 end will be 78% of 50.76 million hectares of minor irrigation potential (Vide item 2 Column 8 of the above Table 3B) which is 39.59 million hectares. Hence, surface water potential under minor irrigation utilised is 50.76–39.59 = 11.17 million hectares.

ii. As soon as a well is drilled or dug, the farmers make all arrangements to utilise water for irrigation, there is very little time gap between creation of irrigation potential and its utilisation under groundwater sector. Therefore, 39.59 million hectares also becomes groundwater potential created under minor irrigation. From item 2 of Column 5 of Table 3B, we know that minor irrigation potential created is 59.04 million hectares. Since, 59.04 million hectares includes groundwater potential, which we have seen is 39.59 million hectares.

iii. Therefore, surface water minor irrigation potential created is 59.04-39.59 = 19.45 million hectares against which as seen from note i) above the utilisation is 11.17 million hectares.

Despite the above noted progress, we cannot ignore certain distressing aspects of irrigation situation. We are heading towards water stress conditions, if not, crisis on the irrigation front. On the one hand, groundwater tables are depleting fast; in Punjab, Haryana, western Uttar Pradesh and Tamil Nadu and also in some other states; due to over exploitation of groundwater. On the other hand, with the injudicious use of canal water, a considerable extent of cultivable area in agriculturally advanced states is suffering from waterlogging and salinity problems. According to Ministry of Agriculture's (MOA's) estimates the area affected by waterlogging alone in the country is 8.5 million hectares. It is also estimated by the MOA that 36% of irrigated area or 20 million hectares is affected by salinity problems in the country (vide Evaluation of Drip Irrigation Systems (under centrally sponsored scheme for use of plastics in agriculture) sponsored by Department of Agriculture Cooperation, GOI and National Committee on Use of Plastics in Agriculture) by Agricultural Finance Corporation, Mumbai, Northern Regional Office, New Delhi, October 1998 – Chapter 1 p.1. That is, 28.5 million hectares are affected by salinity and related problems, which includes alkalinity. Considering these problems GOI has sponsored schemes under Command Area Development Authority (CADA) for reclamation of waterlogged and saline and alkaline lands. Every year these lands are being reclaimed. These 28.5 million hectares were noted in study conducted in 1998 and therefore, they might relate to years around mid-1990s. Considering that each year 5% of the area is reclaimed from mid-1090s to 2005, ten years would have lapsed. Therefore, at least 50% of the area or 14.25 million hectares is estimated to have been reclaimed.

The remedy of recharge of groundwater table lies in universal coverage of watershed management technology which is described elsewhere in detail in this report.

Another warning signal which emerges is that minor irrigation potential created under surface water was 19.45 million hectares (vide note iii above); out of this the potential utilised is only 11.17 million hectares or 57%! This is due to the fact that many minor irrigation works are not in a proper order of repair. A detailed description is given under the section on maintenance ahead.

It needs to be mentioned that such a valuable asset as irrigation created and utilised should not be lost by our policies of injudicious use. We should jealously protect these assets and expeditiously reclaim what we have lost.

From the inferences given in Table 3B, the following Tables (3C, 3D, 3E) emerge.

Table 3C
Irrigation potential created and utilised from surface water sources up to March end 2005

(Million hectares)

Sl No.	Item	Major/Medium	Minor	Total
1.	Potential created	40.28	19.45	59.73
2.	Potential utilised	33.13	11.17	44.30
3.	% of potential utilised to potential created	82.00	57.00	74.00

Challenges on Irrigation Front

Table 3D summarises performance up to March end 2005 vis a vis ultimate irrigation potential of India, to be created deploying traditional method of Flood/Flow method of irrigation (FMI)

Thus, the reported utilisation will be 83.89/99.32 x 100 = 84%; but actual utilisation will be 69.64/99.32 x 100 = 70%.

Thereby the challenges before us are as under:

1. to utilise irrigation potential already created.
2. to reclaim irrigation potential, which has been lost due to salinity and waterlogging problems.

3. to create and utilise fresh irrigation potential from the ultimate potential of 140 million hectares, i.e. 140–99.32 = 40.68 million hectares.

Table 3D

Irrigation Potential ultimate vs potential created and potential utilised classified according to surface water and groundwater up to end of March 2005 using FMI

(million hectares)

Sl No		Item	Surface water	Ground water	Total area
1.		* Ultimate irrigation potential	76.00	64.00	140.00
2.		Potential created up to March 2005 end	59.73	39.59 **	99.32
3	i	Reported Potential utilised up to end of March 2005	44.30	39.59 **	83.89
	ii.	Of the reported potential utilised area affected by salinity/waterlogging up to end March 2005 (potential lost)	14.25	–	14.25
	iii	Actual irrigation potential utilised up to end March 2005 (item i - ii)	30.05	39.59	69.64
4.		Reported potential yet to be utilised from potential created up to end March 2005 (item 2 – 3 i)	15.43	–	15.43
5.		Actual potential yet to be utilised i.e. reported potential yet to be utilised+ potential lost (item 3 ii + item 4)	29.68	–	29.68
6.		Potential yet to be created considering ultimate irrigation potential as at the end of March 2005 (item 1 – item	16.27	24.41	40.68

* Taskforce Report of Shri Suresh P. Prabhu

** As per note i below Table 3B

Table 3E
Irrigation potential created and utilised from groundwater sources classified according to area served by wells/borewells with IP sets and without IP sets

Sl No.	Item	Area Million hectares	Source
1.	Groundwater potential created and utilised up to March end 2005	39.59	Table 3D
2.	Of the potential in item 1 above that which is served by IP sets	12.69	Notes below
3.	Groundwater potential created and utilised without IP sets (1-2)	26.90	

Notes: According to Inter-State Economic Indicators brought out by Planning Department (PFR Division), Government of Karnataka May 2004, IP sets energised were 13.04 million or 13 million as on 31 March 2002. Considering that some of the IP sets are used for drinking water and some for lift irrigation and also taking into account increases up to March 2005, a modest estimate of 12.69 million IP sets is made for being used for irrigation as at the end of March 2005. Each well with an IP set by conventional method of irrigation will irrigate about 1 hectare. Hence, the above estimate of 12.69 million hectare.

Creation and Utilisation of Irrigation Potential

Another distressing factor is the time gap between creation of irrigation potential and its utilisation. The Tenth FYP target itself indicates that the target for creation of irrigation potential was 16.75 million hectares (vide Table 3); while target for utilisation was 11.63 million hectares (vide Table 3A). What is more surprising is that we were left with non-utilisation of 14 million hectares for which potential was created as at the end of Nineth FYP (end of March 2002 vide note 4 under Table 2). But we have in the Tenth FYP targeted to create an irrigation potential of 16.75 million hectares and utilise 11.63 million hectares as per targets of Tenth FYP. If we consider 14 million hectares of spillover potential created but not yet utilised as at the end of Nineth FYP then we will be leaving a spillover of unutilised potential of 14+16.75–11.63 = 14+5.12 = 19.12 million hectares of created potential left unutilised as at the end of Tenth FYP or at the end of March 2007 even if the Tenth FYP targets are fully met! It is as if we are planning for greater spillover of non-utilised potential. Therefore, the target fixation should have been a number which is at least above 14 million hectares for utilisation in Tenth FYP but as seen from above it is not so. In planning for utilisation in the future plans, we should ensure that the backlog of potential created but not utilised should be covered and also the coverage should extend to what is targeted for creation in the future plan. In fact, there should also be targets for reclaiming potential utilised but lost due to salinity-related problems and waterlogging; otherwise the figures of utilisation will not be reflecting actual utilisation of irrigation potential as we have seen from notes below Table 3D.

Groundwater Creation/Utilisation of Irrigation Potential

Insofar as groundwater is concerned, there is no time lag between creation and utilisation of irrigation potential. This happens simply because both the creation and utilisation is in the hands of private farmers who will not invest for creation of a well and wait indefinitely for the waters to be utilised. In fact, the estimate for creation of the well will also involve estimates for levelling land, drawing field irrigation channels and even working out ways of draining surplus water if any. Therefore, what all is created as irrigation potential as groundwater has to be taken as irrigation potential utilised also. This point has been made very clear in note i and ii below Table 3B. The potential created under groundwater and utilised as at the end of March 2005 is 39.59 million hectares.

3

Costs of Creation and Utilisation of Irrigation Potential

Another factor, which generally gets ignored, is the heavy cost that is incurred by the government in the creation of surface water irrigation potential, which gets locked up till it is utilised, for which, only small loan component from financial institutions or cooperative sector is called for. The relative costs for creation of irrigation potential and utilisation of potential created are given below to indicate the same.

In Karnataka state the costs of creation of irrigation potential both for ongoing and completed projects is given below as on 31 March 2001.

Table 4
Cost of creating irrigation potential up to end of March 2001
(Major/Medium Irrigation Projects)

Sl No.	Item	Cost/estimated cost (Rs in lakhs)	Potential created (lakh hectares)	Cost per hectare (Rs)
1.	8 Major and 34 Medium project completed as on 31-3-2001	167	4.57	3,654
2.	21 major and 19 medium ongoing projects beyond 31-3-2001	19,270	23.41	82,315
	Total	19,437	27.98	69,468

(Vide First of the Revenue Reforms Commission, Government of Karnataka, First Report, Volume 1, November 2003, p. 313)

The cost per hectare for creating irrigation potential was Rs 69,468 per hectare up to March 2001 since inception. Taking increase in cost into account the costs in 2005 for creating 1 hectare of potential under surface water are taken as Rs 1.25 lakh per hectare. This can be taken as cost per hectare across the board for minor irrigation also since out of 140 million hectares of ultimate irrigation potential, the potential yet to be created from surface water is only 16.27 million hectares. Therefore, under minor irrigation there will be only very little area. Hence, the above cost per hectare will represent major/medium and minor irrigation.

Cost of Utilisation of Irrigation Potential

Utilisation of irrigation potential takes place in the fields, if Field Irrigation Channels (FIC) and Field Drainage Channels (FDC) are constructed and On Farm Development (OFD) involving land levelling is undertaken. Thus, there are three distinct components of work to be carried out for utilisation to take place. There are variations noticed in terms of area for these three components as given by CADA in Table 5. This has happened because some areas might have developed FICs or FDCs or OFDs or either two or three of them together. In any case as assessed by all the CADAs of Karnataka up to March 2003, Table 5 indicates costs of various components of work to be carried out for utilisation to result in.

Table 5
Utilisation of Irrigation Potential – Componentwise cost (Command Area Development Works as on March 2003)

Sl no.	Component of work	Area covered in lakh hectares	Cost (Rs Crores)	Cost per hectare (Rs)	Cost of each component as percent of total cost
1.	Field irrigation channels	21.20	1,224.51	5,776	51
2.	Field drainage channels	12.73	96.30	757	7
3.	On farm development works	20.30	926.19	4,740	42
	Total cost per hectare	–	–	11,273	100

(vide report of First Revenue Reforms Commission Vol –I November 2003 p. 390)

The above cost relate to utilisation of irrigation potential if, conventional methods of irrigation (i.e. FMI) is considered. In Appendix 7 detailed cost estimates for various requirements of usage of irrigation potential have been worked out and projected.

The ultimate irrigation potential, potential created and potential utilised up to the end of the Tenth Plan as envisaged by Planning Commission, GOI – Eleventh FYP 2007-2012 is given in Table 6:

Table 6
Ultimate Irrigation Potential, Potential Created and Potential Utilised

(in million hectares)

Sector	Ultimate Irrigation Potential	Potential Created		Potential Utilised	
		Till End of Nineth Plan	Anticipated in Tenth Plan	Till end of Nineth Plan	Anticipated in Tenth Plan
MMI	58.47	37.05	5.3	31.01	3.41
MI					
Surface water	17.38	13.6	0.71	11.44	0.56
Groundwater	64.05	43.3	2.81	38.55	2.26
Subtotal	81.43	56.9	3.52	49.99	2.82
Total	139.9	93.95	8.82	81.00	6.23

(Source: Planning Commission, GOI, Eleventh FYP 2007-12)

4

Task Force Proposal on Interlinking of Inter-basin Rivers

The Task Force chaired by Shri Suresh P. Prabhu on Interlinking of Rivers, Ministry of Water Resources, GOI, New Delhi, 2003, has given inter-basin water transfer proposal, as mentioned below:

1. The estimated foodgrain requirement by AD 2050, when the population of the country will stabilise at 1,640 million or 164 crore, will be 450 million tonnes.
2. With foreseeable improvement in food production, it is anticipated that foodgrain crop yields will improve from AD 2010 to AD 2050 as under:

Table 7
Yield per hectare tonnes

Year	Rain fed	Irrigated
2010	1.1	3.0
2050	1.5	4.0

3. The required 450 million tonnes, has to be produced from net cultivable area, which is 143 million hectares, which may go up to 145 million hectares. The limit of availability of land for cultivation has already been reached.

4. The ultimate irrigation potential is 140 million hectares. Hence, this may lead to substantial shortages of foodgrain production. Shortages and large scale import of foodgrains is likely to be, socially unacceptable.
5. Inter-basin water transfer based on proven technology, has a potential of 35 million hectares of additional irrigation potential, of which 10 million hectares will be groundwater potential due to excess seepage on account of inter-basin transfer. This will lead to 175 million hectares as our ultimate irrigation potential.
6. To be able to produce 450 million tonnes of foodgrains, it is necessary to put land under food crops in the non-monsoon season, which can be done through irrigation.
7. With 175 million hectares under irrigation, attempts need to be made, to be not only satisfied with producing enough to eat, but the strategy needs to be to produce surplus for export to achieve a commanding position. Therefore, considering both internal consumption and exports, the country has to plan for 550 million tonnes of foodgrain production by AD 2050.
8. Long distance inter-basin transfer is not a new concept and has been in practice in India for over five centuries. The Periyar project, Parambikulam Aliyar project, Kurnool-Cuddapah canal and Telugu Ganga project, have been cited as good examples of inter-basin transfer of water in South India. Similarly, in North India inter-sub-basin transfers in Indus basin and Rajasthan canal project are some of the projects executed in the nineteenth and twentieth centuries. Inter-sub-basin transfers in the basin, have a diversion dam Pandoh 140 km upstream of Pong dam on Beas river, which enables diversion of water from Beas to Bhakra reservoir on Sutlej river and generates 165 mw of power on the way. The Beas-Sutlej link is 37.25 km long of which 25.45 km is tunnel, through difficult rock formations. The Rajasthan canal diverts water from the Himalayas to deserts of Rajasthan. The project comprises of a huge multipurpose project constructed across Beas River at Pong, a barrage at Harike and a Grand Canal system. These interlinking projects both in South and North India have been highly beneficial and have not resulted in any noticeable environmental damages.

All the above views of the Task Force are practical and can be implemented; and thereby additional 35 million hectares of irrigation potential can be created with 34,000 mw of hydropower.

But, the Task Force itself admits that inter-basin water transfer proposals, by their very nature are complex. This transfer, is a product of the hydrologic and engineering complexities of the plan of operation and further the legal, social, political and economic issues are involved. Naturally, a plan of this magnitude will require considerable time for its implementation. But with intra-basin water which is largely available now, with which we hope to reach an ultimate irrigation potential of 140 million hectares by present system of conventional flow irrigation method, under which water is supplied from sources of storage like reservoir, etc., via canals, distributaries, sub-distributaries, laterals, water courses, etc., to the fields involve considerable wastage of water by seepage and evaporation. The same quantity of water, if it is economically used greater extent of land can be brought under irrigation. Alternate methods of economically delivering water to the plants and not to the fields are available and have to be used in greater interest of the nation. The same are discussed in the next chapter.

5

Alternate Possibilities of Additional Irrigation Potential Through Economic Use of Water

What the Task Force has spoken of, substantially relates to diversion of water from areas of surplus to deficit areas, by inter-basin transfer mechanism; which we certainly should avail in course of time. Let us at the same time, explore savings of water which can result, consequent to application of water saving devices like sprinkler and drip, which have in them the potential not merely of saving water but also, increasing efficiency of water use for increasing production per unit of water, by delivering water to the plant, compared to the flood or FMI, which is now conventionally practised in India, under which water is delivered to the land where plants are grown. Only in very few individual fields, where people have cared to instal these devices largely with subsidies, these are being used. The following is a comparative study of systems deploying sprinkler or drip compared with the conventional FMI.

Comparative study of FMI versus SMI and DMI is given below:

Flow or Flood Method of Irrigation (FMI)

The existing conventional system of FMI of irrigation entails heavy losses both in evaporation and distribution. It consists of application of water to the field and not to the crop. At one time during each rotation of water supply, irrespective of actual requirement of water by the crop, it delivers 8-10 cm of water to the fields. There is thus, wastage of water by way of percolation and evaporation. The crop also remains under stress, during half the rotation period. The low efficiencies in use of water under this system lead to soil erosion, salination and waterlogging. Hence, the average yield of the crop is reduced substantially. According to MOA, GOI estimates, the area affected by waterlogging is 8.5 million hectares and that affected by salinity is 20 million hectares vide evaluation of drip irrigation system, sponsored by Department of Agriculture and Cooperation and National Committee on the use of plastics in agriculture conducted by Agricultural Finance Corporation Ltd., Mumbai and its Northern Regional Office, New Delhi, October 1998, hereinafter to be called Study No.1 in this report. We have already discussed how attempts are being made through government schemes implemented by CADAs, to reclaim the land affected by waterlogging/salinity related problems. There is always fear of further land being affected by these problems, unless totally new systems of irrigation are introduced under which possibility of repetition of such problems is ruled out. The micro irrigation systems discussed below are such systems.

Micro-Irrigation Systems

As against the traditional water supply method of FMI, under which water is supplied through canals distributaries, sub-distributaries, lateral, and then delivered to field irrigation channels to supply water to the fields and not the crop. Micro-irrigation systems, comprising usage of sprinklers and drips apply water in a controlled manner directly to the plant as and when required. The quantum of water so supplied is tailored to the requirement of the crop at different stages of growth. Let us see below a description of these two systems.

1. Sprinkler Method of Irrigation (SMI)

The invention and development of modern means of lifting water and progress in application of light weight, non-corrosive metals and plastics for the manufacture of pipes have fostered the development of this overhead water supply system of irrigation. Its concept, practice and efficiency is far ahead of the traditional method of surface flow irrigation (i.e FMI) in terms of water use efficiency, adaptability, crop production, etc. Sprinkler irrigation, is based on the principle that water is delivered under high pressure into a system of portable, light weight, quick-coupling irrigation lines with sprinklers mounted at regular intervals. A wide choice of sprinklers designed, mounted for operation under various distribution and flow characteristics make this rain-like irrigation system adaptable to a wide range of agricultural conditions and crops.

Since under SMI crop is irrigated by overhead sprinklers, which can be either stationery or mobile, this system has lot of flexibility. This method, has only one limitation, viz., wind direction which plays a major role, whereby excess irrigation in direction of wind occurs, as against the area which is opposed to the wind direction; the sprinkler does have an advantage in closely staged crops such as cereals, soyabean and vegetable crops. Thus, for these crops, sprinklers are very suitable.

Saving of Water

Sprinklers are now being used in India and subsidy is also offered by the government. Sprinklers are being constantly modified and their construction and hydraulic performance improved. The quick coupling units have now been made stronger and less corrosive, couplers are made to operate more under a wide range of pressures and pumps are designed to suit the hydraulic characteristics of the system.

In a feasibility report for 'Comprehensive Land Use Management Project' for Harkanhal Mandal, Bellary District, Karnataka State, conducted by M/s Agricultural Finance Consultants Ltd., Bombay, January 1989, water savings have been estimated as under.

Installing sprinklers on all ten minor irrigation tanks with an *achakat* of 325.44 hectares was proposed. The water from the tanks was proposed to be conveyed to a jack well by using hume pipes instead of open channels (to avoid losses due to seepage and evaporation). From the jack well water could be pumped via suitable pipe system for sprinklers to work. The estimated achakat with sprinkler use is indicated as 700 hectares, i.e. 215% rise or an increase of 115% in achakat and consequent saving in water.

In the above case, of SMI the feasibility study of Harkanhal Mandal water saving is effected by saving of water, which would have been wasted in canals, etc., by drawing through hume pipes from the tanks direct to the jack wells in the fields, from where it is lifted by pipes and delivered via sprinkler to plants. Thus, the saving is indicated as 115%. This 115% increase in achakat is seen if water was drawn by hume pipes from the tank up to the field. But generally in major-medium or in minor irrigation works also the water flows to the fields via canals, distributaries, laterals, and field irrigation channels and thereby considerable water is wasted. The feasibility study of Harangi project in Karnataka state has considered these losses of water supplied through canals, etc., as 45%. In fact, if this water, which is supplied via canals, distributaries, sub-distributaries, laterals, is let out and is received by pipes instead of field irrigation channels under conventional method, and stored in a storage place on ground or elevated location and from there if water is pumped to sprinklers there will be at least 115–45 = 70% more achakat. Let us conservatively put this water saving and increase in achaket due to use of sprinklers as 50%. Thus, there will be no wastage of water and the sprinkler systems will bring about at least 50% saving of water. The soil is also not eroded and does not become saline since it is not flooded with water.

2. Drip Method Irrigation (DMI)

Drip is the latest method of irrigation. It is also known as 'trickle irrigation'. It is primarily a water saving method. Under drip system water is dripped at the roots of the plants, thereby avoiding loss of water either by way of evaporation or seepage.

During early 1940, Symcha Blass, an Israeli engineer observed that a large tree near a leaking faucet exhibited a more vigorous growth compared with other trees in the area. This led him to the concept of irrigation system that would apply water in small amounts, literally drop-by-drop. The technique as developed was subsequently refined by Blass and other manufacturers. One of the refinements Blass made in his original system was a coiled emitter. It consisted of a spiral tube in a hard casing. The tube served to reduce the discharge pressure by strengthening the flow path of water, thereby making it possible to discharge water at low pressure while dripping.

installation of the system. This resulted in unsatisfactory performance of a large number of drip systems installed under the scheme especially in areas where expertise for their operation and maintenance was locally not available. This obviously put the farmers to undue hardship and may be the reason for intensity being found only in 20 districts of the states mentioned above because more drip systems in a place will attract more repairers and other experts.

6. Yield Increase due to Use of Drips

1. Barring banana and citrus which registered 41% increase in yield, the yield increase in other crops was grapes 81%, coconut 116%, mango 76%.
2. The recovery climate was good with hardly any case of default due to the highly remunerative nature of the investment.
3. The quality of the produce will also be better because water is delivered at the time when it is needed by the plant and the plant is not unnecessarily stressed by excess supply of water; and the produce will qualify as high grade and hence, will secure higher price per unit produce.

7. Cost Benefit

The Indian National Committee on Irrigation and Drainage constituted by the Ministry of Water Resources, GOI brought out in July 1994 a comprehensive publication on drip irrigation in India. The major finding was that the entire fixed cost on the system ranged from Rs 18,000 per hectare in case of pomegranate to Rs 32,500 per hectare in case of chillies, cucumber and grapes. This cost including drip and accessories + motor and accessories was far lower than the net incremental income during one season accruing from any one of the above crops taken with the use of the system. Table 8 below brings out the net extra income due to installation of the drip system over conventional method of irrigation as given in Table 8:

Table 8
Net Extra Income due to drip irrigation system

(Rs per hectares)

Crop	Incremental Income
Banana	2,62,600-00
Chillies	73,220-00
Cucumber	33,335-00
Grapes	4,95,435-00
Mosambi	2,11,400-00
Pomegranate	1,40,628-00
Tomato	62,660-00
Watermelon	1,22,670-00

8. Another Study

Micro-irrigation for sugarcane: The research experiments conducted in Vasant Dada Sugar Institute Manjari (Maharashtra)-VASI and operational research trails at different cooperative sugar factories in Maharashtra State indicate that, drip irrigation has the greatest potential in saving irrigation water and increasing sugarcane yield and thereby water use efficiency. The highlights of this research were summarised in a paper entitled 'Drip Irrigation in Sugarcane-Care and Maintenance' circulated at national level training programme on sustainable development of sugarcane based cropping system sponsored by GOI and organised at the institute in February 1997. These are reproduced below for ready reference.

Table 9
Benefits of Drip Irrigation in Sugarcane

Sl No.	Item	Observation
1	Water Saving	50–55%
2	Increase in yield	25-30%
3	Water use efficiency compared to conventional irrigation	2-2.5 times more

Table contd...

4	Best suited planting system	Paired row system (0.75 m x 1.35m)
5	Fertiliser saving	25-30%
6	Saving cost of cultivation	About 20%
7	Best suited drip system in sugarcane	Surface drip system with pressure compensating drippers

Thus, water saving can be safely taken as 50% in drip also although water use efficiency will make it higher (All the above observations 1 – 8 have been obtained from Study No. 1). Saving in fertiliser mentioned in item 5 of Table 9 will be there since fertiliser is mixed with water and supplied via pipes to the root sone in drip irrigation.

Although no evaluation study of sprinkler except one could be cited but the problems encountered and the performance in saving water and costs and increasing benefits are more or less the same for sprinkler system also as for drip.

Savings of Water

From a perusal of the above discussion we can safely conclude that, installing drip or sprinkler will save at least 50% of water compared to the conventional FMI. Even if the water is brought through canals, distributaries, laterals, etc., up to the field and from the field level instead of field irrigation channels pipes take over the waters to the storage place in the field and thereafter pipes take the water to drip and sprinklers systems for supply to plants, but only extra cost will be cost of power in case of surface water also, which is discussed ahead in this report.

Increase in Production

From the above discussion we have seen that minimum increase will be 30% in yield per hectare, if these water saving devices are used although we have seen in many cases it will be much more.

Saving of Cost of Cultivation

The cost of cultivation will be less because; fertiliser and pesticides will be passed through water, which flows through the pipes to the sprinklers and drip systems to deliver the same to the plant. Saving in wages on application of fertiliser/pesticide will also result. Further, the cost of weeding will also minimal because water flow through pipes does not allow weeds to grow. If at all due to rain, etc., some weeds are grown the cost of de-weeding will be far too low.

Improvement in Quality of Products

It has been observed that, due to regulated supply of water to the plants and not to the field under sprinkler and drip systems quality of produce is improved, whereas flood irrigation causes stress on the plants reducing the quality. If the quality of produce is better, it qualifies for better gradation at market level and securing higher prices per unit of produce.

Mass Production and Reduction of Costs

All that we are noticing in the usage of sprinkler or drip in India is largely due to governmental subsidy and hence has limitations. So far as GOI subsidy for drip is concerned, it is as high as 70% for drip for general category of farmers and 90% for SC/ST farmers. We have seen that, with all the subsidy support as on 1 April 1998 only 3 lakh hectare were covered under drip system of which 62% was the coverage with central subsidy, 19% with Maharashtra State subsidy and 19% with farmers' investment. Further, if massive use of sprinklers and drips is made, mass production will take place and the investment cost for installing drip and sprinklers will be considerably reduced. As we have seen earlier, this is already a bankable proposition as per Study No. 1. Financial institutions will certainly come forward to support this programme.

Strong Case for Universal Use of Drip/Sprinkler Systems

As we have seen, without usage of drip or sprinkler, even the irrigation facility we have created is being lost due to waterlogging and salinity in FMI. In utilisation of irrigation potential utilised to the extent of about 57 million hectares net, which we have created up to 1998-99 (vide Table 11 ahead), the loss of 20 million hectares by salination and 8.5 million hectares by waterlogging totalling to 28.5 million hectares that to by 1998 as assessed by MOA, GOI as we have stated elsewhere above, is a great loss. (It is almost 50% loss of net irrigation potential of 57 million hectares reported to be under use by the year 1998-99).

Therefore first, there is need to reclaim the saline and waterlogged lands and make our irrigated achakat salinity proof and waterlogging proof by universal use of drip/sprinkler method of irrigation. This type of proofing against salinity and waterlogging can be done only by adopting SMI and DMI methods of irrigation universally. In addition we have seen that minimum saving of water for irrigation will be as much as 50% if these devices are used. Therefore, our ultimate irrigation potential can go beyond 140 million hectares, i.e. by minimum 50% more. Thus 140+70 = 210 million hectares will be our ultimate irrigation potential (which includes area sown more than once), even with present availability of water. The production will increase on an average by 30% in quantity with better quality of produce fetching better price per unit produce. All this can be done without even carrying out inter-basin transfer of water, which is proposed by GOI Task Force on linking inter-basin rivers. Actually as and when Task Force proposals materialise and additional water becomes available, this will be an addition to our water supply requirements.

The pathetic performance with availability of so much subsidy of coverage of only 3 lakh hectares under drip as on 1 April 1998 when work started from the early 1980s is another warning signal. In fact, when we consider the fact that we became aware of this technology in 1960 and then confined it to research institutes till 1980, it speaks of our poor response to newer technologies in the agriculture sector. The strategy of taking up these systems (SMI and DMI) should be changed from subsidy-based to industry-based, since subsidies have extended the area only to 3 lakh hectares from over 57 million hectares of net irrigated land in 1998-99! Therefore, impact of this technology is negligible. In other words, subsidies should be abolished and universal use of these water saving devices should be adopted, then industry will find opportunity to appropriately expand its production capacity to meet the massive demand for these devices at a cheaper rate. Thus, industry-oriented spread of drip and sprinkler for utilisation of our waters will take place. And, we have seen that knowledge of use of drip is given more by industry than government departments as per Study No. 1. Although some reputed industries are there in the field, just like M/s Jain Irrigation Systems Ltd. which AFCs evaluation Study No. 1 calls it as a flagship company having been established in 1987 has played a pioneering role in promoting drip systems in Maharashtra. But, various traders also have entered the fray, simply because government subsidy is available and they can make efforts to sell systems manufactured by others. These traders, who are not manufacturers, will not be of long-term use in providing backup repair services.

Now, big groups like Reliance have also started taking interest in sprinklers.

For Sprinkler irrigation, RIL (Reliance Industries Limited) has designed inside-smooth-lining coated (RELPIPE XFLOTM) polyethylene pipes that claim less energy consumption. According to a company spokesperson: 'This ensures that the farmers can use low HP pump sets to deliver the same amount of irrigation water. The sprinkler pipes are already popular in Vidarbha (Maharashtra), AP and MP. Also, the fitting systems are so developed that the water leakages are totally eliminated, thus allowing full value for money.'

He goes on to claim, 'That's not all. Unlike other rigid pipes such as PVC used in the field, RELPIPES need not be buried under the ground as they are unaffected by continuous exposure to sun and other elements of nature. These pipes along with its light weightlessness enables farmers to shift the pipeline after a given irrigation cycle from one area to another. As the farmer need not bury the pipeline under the soil, he can use lesser number of pipes. Also, the farmer can loan or share the pipeline with his co-farmers. This particular type of irrigation is not popular in India but we at Reliance are promoting the same to ensure lesser capital expenditure, which is a boon to marginal and small farmers.'

We have also seen that efforts in isolated places to use sprinkler/drip suffer from repair and service facilities and even for replacement of worn out parts, the farmers may have to travel long distances to meet their needs in this behalf. We have seen that not merely water is saved but due to controlled and regulated supply of water to plants (not to fields as in the case of conventional systems) at the right time in each stage of plant growth, we are in a position to supply water economically, which results in substantial increase of quantity and quality of the produce, thereby resulting in better returns to the farmers.

(Vide 'Irrigation Equipment' published in Agriculture and Industries Survey, Vol no.14, Issue no. 8, 2004 by their correspondent)

The traditional method of irrigation in India (i.e FMI) has to undergo a thorough and universal change. The methodology for installing these systems under various types of irrigation is given in Chapter 6.

6

Methodology for Change From Conventional Method of Irrigation to Sprinkler and Drip Systems, and Maintenance System

Major/Medium Irrigation Surface Water

In major/medium works, water flows through canals, branch canals, distributaries, sub-distributaries and laterals. At the laterals at 1-cusec level of water flow, it is taken by field irrigation channels prepared by farmers and delivered to plants in properly levelled fields, and surplus water is drained off by FDCs which join the main drain created for the village or group of villages. In case drainage systems are not properly constructed or maintained because the farmers are more interested in letting in the water than letting it out, then salinity, alkalinity and waterlogging occurs. We have noticed that substantial chunks of lands in command areas of major/medium irrigation projects are affected by these maladies. In case we introduce drip/ sprinkler systems then instead of receiving the water delivered from laterals at 1-cusec level by FICs, it would be taken by pipes of proper size to a storage place on ground or at an elevated place which will supply water by pipes to four or five fields if they are small or to one field if it is big. Then, from the storage place, water is supplied by pipes to each small field or to one big field as the case may be. This storage place could be a storage tank on ground or an elevated storage tank, from where water stored, will be supplied to the plants by the drip or sprinkler arrangement on water supply pipes made in the field. In all these places low HP motors will be used. In case of drip, no water or very little water may fall in the field in addition to rainwater and in case of sprinkler some water may fall and in addition, there will be rainwater in the field for being drained through drainage channels, which should be kept intact in the fields. In lands which are utilising water now, the developments that exist now like OFD may be kept intact and only difference is that at the entry point in the field, water will be taken by pipes instead of FICs and delivered to a storage place from where it is taken by pipes to drip/sprinkler systems for delivery to plants. Only care of drainage channels is to be taken. If these channels need repair or renovation, that should be done. If they do not exist they should be provided and linked to main drain. Linkage to main drain on the part of all field drains is important. It should also be seen that repairs if any for the main drains should also be carried out. Otherwise, salinity or alkalinity or waterlogging will take place destroying irrigation we have created. Another essential requirement will be installation of a meter and pressure gauge at the point where water is received in pipes in each field, so as to enable measured quantity of water delivered to the field.

In lands where potential is created but not yet utilised, FICs will not be necessary because, by pipes water will be supplied to storage places and from then on pipes will feed the sprinkler and drip sets which will supply water to the plants, but land levelling, under OFD and FDCs have to be prepared and the FDCs should be connected to the main drain of the area. In fact, whenever it rains, part of the precipitation has to go down the drain and for that also FDCs will be necessary. In case of DMI, even in undulating terrains crops can be grown, but still certain degree of levelling may be needed to drain rainwater from fields via drainage channels. Thus, OFD will have to be suitably modified wherever SMI and DMI systems are taken up and it will cost lesser than conventional method. A meter may be installed at the entry point where water is received in each field which will give us the reading of quantity of water used periodically during each season for assessing water rates. One more factor which is already explained is that an elevated storage tank for 4 to 5 farmers could also be prepared and water supplied therefrom via pipes fitted with sprinklers and drips to the plants in various fields. But this has to be jointly maintained. And, at supply point of each farmers field a meter could be installed to measure received quantity of water. Since a large number of farmers are small and marginal farmers, this method appears to be suitable. But, however, where holdings are medium or large, single elevated tank for each farmer could be considered, as has been discussed earlier.

Maintenance

The maintenance of major medium irrigation projects relates to maintenance of catchment areas, the reservoirs and dam, the distribution system and the command area.

Catchment Areas

So far as the catchment areas of reservoirs are concerned, they are all macro watersheds. The watershed technology consists of revival of vegetative growth from ridgeline of hillocks and uplands down to the plains. In cultivable lands, contour bunding of cultivable lands so as to prevent flow of silt is undertaken. The streams and small *nallas* which are the feeder channels to the reservoirs have also become silted up and vegetative growth has also taken place along their courses. These streams are to be de-silted and de-vegetated. Further, check dams should be built on these feeder channels so as to prevent the flow of silt but, allow overflow of water over the check dams in the rainy seasons, so that only water reaches the reservoirs and not the silt. This has been described in great detail elsewhere under a specific section written for watershed management. Funding for this has to come from river valley schemes as well as National Rural Employment Guarantee Act (NREGS) and other rural employment schemes more particularly, watershed schemes, which are taken up specifically to carry out watershed management with meticulous details. As stated, these are described elsewhere in detail. This remedy will almost slow down the flow of silt into the reservoirs that it becomes nearer to nil flow. In fact, when the Revenue Reforms Commission of the Government of Karnataka visited the Tungabadra project, the secretary, Thungabadra Board presented certain figures before the Commission which indicted that in the few recent years the flow of silt had come down. This was the result of the Thungabadra River Valley Scheme of carrying out afforestation in up lands and contour bunding in cultivable lands. Thus, this work is very beneficial for avoiding siltation of the reservoirs. This type of watershed management will also minimise flow of silt through the feeder channels to the reservoirs.

Dams

The maintenance of dams is of prime importance. The Central Water Commission and the state governments have their own procedure of inspecting the dams and these should be adhered to meticulously. Unfortunately, in Karnataka recently, at the Almatti Dam in Upper Krishna Project, during the prime rainy season, the gates of the dam created some problems. This appears to be due to the failure of the maintenance systems in vogue. Care should be taken to see that not a single procedure is ignored, although in India, so far no major disasters have taken place. Government may release grants whenever required.

Canals

Many times, breaches of the canals come to surface in various major/medium irrigation projects. It calls for greater vigilance and better maintenance by the irrigation departments.

Distributaries/Sub-distributaries

The Revenue Reforms Commission of Government of Karnataka has recommended in its first report (November 2003), that for every lateral covering about 1,000 to 1,500 acres, or 400 to 600 hectares, there should be a WUS. The WUS has to be charged with the responsibility of taking care of the maintenance of the lateral which supplies water to its members. Towards this, the Commission has recommended that the WUS may collect the water rate and credit it to irrigation department. It is necessary, that, at least 10% of these water rates are retained by the WUS to maintain lateral under its charge. The WUS should also be allowed to raise its own resources by carrying out activities like fisheries and growing coconut trees around the canals and distributaries serving them. This will supplement the resources of the WUS. After, retaining 10% the 90% of the water rates should be credited to the irrigation department of the concerned project, which in turn should credit 50% of the water rate to government and retain 40%, at its level to be spent for repairs of canals and distributaries. Again, for each distributory, there should be a Distributory Level Committee (DLC) which should have a chairman elected by Chairmen of all WUS and the chairmen of all WUS should also be members of DLC. And, the official members should be assistant executive engineers, agricultural/horticultural officers and bankers. Such a representative body should be charged with the responsibility of maintenance of the distributaries and from the 40 % of the water rates collected and retained by the project authorities, 20% should vest in the DLC to carry out maintenance of distributaries. The rest of the 20% in the project may be used for maintenance of the canals. Government grants should also supplement the funds required for maintaining distributaries wherever necessary. One time repair of distributaries/laterals should be carried out by government before they are handed over to DLCs/WUSs, respectively.

Project Level Coordination Committee

At the project level also under the chairmanship of the chief engineer concerned, there should be a project level coordination committee which should have members elected from the chairmen of the various DLCs and all other concerned officials from agriculture and horticulture departments, banks, etc. Such a body of elected representatives and responsible officials should be in the overall charge of maintenance of the dam, canals and distributaries. This committee should also take care of the needs of cropping pattern and other infrastructure needs. All functions discharged by the CADAs may be entrusted to this committee. The government may consider abolishing CADA, since over the years, so much duplication and replication of work has taken place that, even the irrigation potential created over the years has not been utilised. In the new dispensation when the cultivators and the banks will have to invest huge sums to change from FMI to SMI and DMI pattern of irrigation, the outdated institutions like

CADA will have to be eased out. This coordination committee should also take decisions on optimal use of water and adoption of proper cropping pattern including supply of all inputs in time.

Minor Irrigation (MI) Surface Water

a) Tanks, anicuts etc.

The minor irrigation surface water works like tanks, anicuts, pickups, barrages will supply water through small canals or channels which take water up to the entry point of each field through the channels. From the channels, at the entry point of the field water can be taken by pipes to suitable storage place, viz., storage tank at an elevated place by using low HP motors. And, from the elevated tank water will flow via pipes, drips and sprinkler systems to deliver water to the plants. The meter readings at the entry point of each person's holdings should specify the quantum of water used and thereby the water rate to be paid can be assessed. The land development and drainage suggested for utilisation of water under major/ medium irrigation works will hold good for minor irrigation also. Where, water is already being utilised under minor irrigation care has to be taken to repair the drainage system and on farm development which has already taken place. Needless to say, 4 to 5 farmers joined together can have an elevated tank or the entire ayacut can be served by a big elevated tank. Before sprinkler/drip can be installed and tanks handed over to tank user's societies, one time repair of tanks is to be carried out. A warning signal is already noted by us in this report in notes under Table 3C, wherein, we have noted that 57% of MI potential created is being utilised. The Revenue Reforms Commission of Government of Karnataka in its final report February 2004 has graphically given the various drawbacks from which MI tanks suffer. The tank bunds are reduced to 1 metre width (while at least 2.5 metre width is called for) tank sluices are inoperable with lack of controlling arrangement leading to seepage of water, etc., waste weirs are damaged, canals are to be re-sectioned, re-designed and fully lined so as to prevent transmission losses. Tank beds and feeder channels are silted up. Both curative treatments, by way of desilting and prophylactic measures like watershed treatment in the catchment need to be undertaken. A tank user's committee with chairman elected by the tank users, all tank users being members and official members co-opted could take care of the maintenance, just as in the case of major/medium projects. The other MI works like anicuts, pickups, etc., should also have WUSs. The fund flow given for WUSs of major irrigation projects will apply *mutatis mutandis* to this type of irrigation also.

For Lift Irrigation

For these schemes, the only difference is that, lifted water will be brought by pipes from a stream or a river, etc., and pipes installed in each field or a group of fields will take the water from the main pipes to a storage place at an elevated level in the fields as mentioned earlier, thereafter through sprinkler/drip water can be distributed to plants. At entry point of pipes in the fields, a meter can be installed to assess the quantity of water consumed. The land development and drainage arrangements for utilisation of water suggested for major/medium irrigation will hold good. Only in case of old scheme, it should be ensured that lands are properly levelled and drainage systems are properly repaired. Many government lift irrigation schemes were reported by Karnataka State Revenue Reforms Commission's First Report (November 2003) to be not working or not working properly. The one time repair of these should be carried out and these schemes should be handed over to WUS covered by it. The procedure of maintenance should be the same as in the case of minor irrigation. The fund flow will apply *mutatis mutandis*.

One time repair: In the case of major medium irrigation projects, one time repair of laterals and distributaries may be carried out and handed over to WUS and DLCs to maintain supply systems under their charge. Similarly, for all minor irrigation works one time repair may be carried our before they are handed over to tank/WUSs.

Groundwater

As far as groundwater is concerned, we have seen in the course of this report that, drip sets or sprinklers can be installed by drawing water from wells/borewells with motors to supply water to plants via drip/sprinkler sets.

In case of new borewells or dug wells, wherever motors exists care may be taken to prepare or repair drainage channels and care has to be taken of checking whether land is properly levelled if not, it should be levelled properly. In case of new borewells or dug wells, land shaping has to be done to receive water, drainage systems are to be made. Another advantage of drip irrigation system is that, water drawn from the ground, even if it is saline can be used to grow crops. In the case of drip systems, undulating terrains and also sandy soils can be supplied water to grow suitable crops. In fact, in black cotton soils, which are there in the country in vast extents, the groundwater is saline and cannot be used now. With the prospects of drip irrigation coming in, such water can also be used for crops. Only appropriate land levelling and drainage arrangement will be necessary.

7

Policies towards Land and Water Utilisation, for Cultivation including Cultivation of Foodgrain Crops.

1. Availability of Land for Cultivation

The net sown area between 1998-99 and 1999-2000 has varied between 142.6 million hectares to 141.2 million hectares between the two years, as seen from Table 10 below. But, the Suresh P. Prabhu Task Force has considered the cultivable area as varying between 143 million hectares to 145 million hectares. There is the other cultivable area which can be brought under cultivation, but has been left as waste due to various reasons. At least, the net sown areas plus, the two types of fallow lands (viz., a) current fallow which is cultivable land left as waste during current year and b) five years) could easily be brought under cultivation, since it will not be much difficult to do so. There is also culturable waste land, which is cultivable land left as waste beyond five years. In such an event, the area cultivable will be as shown in table 10.

Table 10
Cultivable area (including fallows & culturable waste)

(in million hectares)

Sl No.	Item	1998-99	1999-2000
1.	Net sown area	142.6	141.2
2.	Fallows		
a)	Current fallow	13.6	14.8
b)	Other fallows	9.9	10.1
c)	Total fallows (2a+2b)	23.5	24.9
3.	Total cultivable land including fallows (1+2C)	166.1	166.1
4.	Culturable waste	13.9	13.8
5.	Total cultivable land including fallows and culturable waste (Item 1+item 2C+item 4)	180.00	179.9

(Vide Appendix 4)

Table 10 clearly brings out the fact that, the cultivable land including fallows will be 166.1 million hectares net. Fallows can easily be brought under cultivation by overcoming reasons due to which, such land was not cultivated. It needs to be stated that, the reasons for non-cultivation of these lands will be simple quarrels in the family leading to litigation, neglect due to poverty or indebtedness, despite land reforms, possession of land holdings by big cultivators in *benami* names, leading to neglect of some lands, etc. So, there should not be any difficulty in using this land (fallow – current and other fallows) which extends over 23.5 million hectares since much of it has been under cultivation within the last five years. Considering all other claims of landuse like forests, grasing lands, land under non-agricultural use (for housing, industry, expansion of cities, etc.); it should not be difficult from 166.1 million hectares to bring at least 150 million hectares under cultivation even though the Task Force on interlinking of inter-basin rivers has assessed the net cultivable land as 145 million hectares, since the micro-hydel systems of DMI/SMI will be able to irrigate that extent of minimum net area in the country.

But, however, we cannot ignore that cultivable wasteland which is also available to us, which is left as waste beyond five years, but still with efforts, it can be brought under cultivation or tree cover. Though such cultivable wasteland, to start with, it could be used for grass in the first year, because soil erosion must have made it unworthy for any cultivation in the first year and some soil binding treatment like growing of grass in the initial stages will be required. In the next year, bush can come up and subsequently tree plantation can take place. In any case, we need tree cover both for improving the environment as well as for generating energy through wood gasifiers. Therefore, cultivable wastelands can be reserved for tree cover, etc.

2. Area Sown more than Once

Table 11 indicates area sown more than once, total cropped area and net sown area.

Table 11

Gross cropped area, net sown area and area sown more than once

(in million hectares)

Sl No.	Item	1998-99	1999-2000
1.	All area (irrigated+unirrigated)		
a.	Gross cropped area	193.0	189.7
b.	Net sown area	142.6	141.2
c.	Area sown more than once	50.4	48.5
d.	Area sown more than once as		
i.	Percentage of net sown area	35.4%	34.3%
ii.	Percentage of gross cropped area	26.1%	26.1%
2.	Irrigated area		
a	Gross irrigated area	75.95	76.33
b	Net irrigated area	57.07	57.24
c	Irrigated area sown more than once	18.88	19.09
d	Irrigated area sown more than once as		
i.	Percentage of net irrigated area	33%	25%
ii.	Percentage of gross irrigated area	33%	25%

(Vide Appendix 4)

Note: item 1 d, 2 c and 2 d have been worked out taking corresponding figures from the appendix cited above. But area sown more than once can increase, provided more water is available.

3. As we have discussed above it will be the policy to limit cultivable land (net) to the extent of 150 million hectares by using a part of the fallow land making it worthy of cultivation.
4. The area under foodgrains during 1996-97 was 123.6 million hectares and during 1997-98 123.8 million hectares (Source: *Inter-State Economic Indicators* brought out by Plan Finance and Resources Division, Planning Department, Government of Karnataka, May 2004). Thus, on an average 123.7 million hectares was the area under foodgrain crops. As against this, the gross cropped area of 193.1 million hectares was there in 1998-99 and 189.7 million hectares in 1999-2000 vide Table 11. The average gross cropped areas of the two years works to 191.35 million hectares. The area under foodgrains of 123.7 million hectares forms 65% of gross cropped area. It should, therefore, be the policy to keep area under foodgrain crop as 65% of gross cropped area.
5. The ultimate irrigation potential of India is 140 million hectares as we have seen from Table 2. Of this ultimate irrigation potential, up to March end 2005 we have utilised 83.89 million hectares (vide Table 3B). But it should be ensured that by 2020, we will utilise 140 million hectares of irrigation potential. If we instal drip and sprinkler irrigation equipment universally, then there will be a saving of minimum 50% of water. That means, the ultimate irrigated area will be 140 + 50/100 x 140 = 140 + 70 = 210 million hectares. Thus, the policy should be to have 210 million hectares as gross cropped area under irrigated cultivation as against 150 million hectares of net cultivated area under irrigation. Thus, 60 million hectares will be area sown more than once against the net 150 million hectares under irrigated cultivation. Thus, area sown more than once will be 60/150 x 100 = 40% for all crops. This will be further facilitated by use of drip and sprinkler irrigation systems universally.
6. Further, all the irrigated land which has become saline or waterlogged in the irrigated areas should be reclaimed by adopting appropriate remedial measures. In fact, we have seen that 20 million hectares have become saline and 8.5 million hectares have become waterlogged. According to the MOA, as per Study No. 1, which was brought out in October 1998. Thus, this wastage of irrigated land is of huge dimension. That is 28.5 million hectares as against 57.07 million hectares of net irrigation

potential in 1998-99 (vide Table 11) or 49.9%, i.e., 50% of net irrigated area! It may be recalled that earlier in this report, we have estimated 14.25 million hectares as the affected area by salinity, alkalinity and waterlogging in 2005, considering efforts of reclamation by CADA. Reclaiming this land and covering all areas including the reclaimed lands under DMI and SMI methods will ensure first, that no area will relapse into salination and waterlogging and sufficient extra water will be available to cover extra land under irrigation. Further, needless to say, no more land will become saline or alkaline because of our policy of universal coverage by these water saving devices.

7. Thus, by 2020, entire anticipated gross cultivated area of 210 million hectares will be covered by irrigation. If gross area is taken as 210 million hectares, then, the area under foodgrain crop will be 65% of 210 = 136.5 million hectares reserved for foodgrain crops.
8. We have seen that the Task Force on inter-linking rivers has projected the production per hectare under foodgrains as under.

The Task Force has mentioned that foodgrain production under rainfed condition will increase from 1.1 tonnes per hectare in 2010 to 1.5 tonnes in 2050 and similarly under-irrigated conditions the foodgrain production per hectare is projected to increase from 3 tonnes in 2010 to 4 tonnes in 2050, keeping all foreseeable improvements in food production. If we can manage to apply all technological improvements, one of them is the usage of drip and sprinkler system, which we have seen increases production by 30%, it should not be difficult to presume that by 2020, production in irrigated land will be 3.5 tonnes per hectare. In that event, the foodgrains production by 2020 will be having 136.5 million hectares x 3.5 tonnes = 478 million tonnes. It may be recalled that the Task Force has stated that 450 million tonnes of foodgrains will be required by 2050, to meet out domestic consumption needs of a stabilised Indian population of 1,640 million people. We know that between 1991-2001, the population grew from 846.3 million to 1,025.2 million or a growth of 21% in the decade. If we project 18% as the decadal increase in population in the next two decades, then by 2021, the population increase will be 36% and actual increased figure will be 1,394 million. If we reduce the 2021 population of 1,394 million by 1.8% which is the projected annual growth, then we will have 1,369 million people in 2020. For 1,369 million population the requirement of foodgrains will be 376 million tonnes (calculated on the basis of the requirement of 450 million tonnes for 1,640 million people, as given by Taskforce). We have seen that we will be producing 478 million tonnes. Thus, we will have foodgrain surplus of 478-376 = 102 million tones in 2020. Actually the Task Force has visualised that by 2050, we will produce 550 million tonnes, while we need 450 million tonnes, i.e a surplus of 100 million tonnes. Thus, in 2020 itself, we are reaching a level of surplus, which is higher than what is needed in 2050. Therefore, lot of surplus will be available for export. Further, as projected by the Task Force, if we reach 4 tonnes per hectare by 2050, we will have a foodgrains production of 136.5 x 4 = 546 million tonnes, which is more than ample to meet the needs of 1,640 million people, which we know is only 450 million tonnes. Thus, we will be in a commanding position to export more foodgrains. In fact, due to 30% increase in production because we propose to use sprinkler/drip systems universally, the production will be 710 million tonnes, which is far beyond what has been anticipated to be reached by conventional type of irrigation by the Task Force, that too, without carrying out inter-basin transfer of river water. The extra water that will become available after carrying out inter-basin transfer of water can be used by us for other purposes like drinking, industries, etc. India will thus become strong both in food and water.

8

Requirement of Power for Micro-Hydel Systems (DMI/SMI)

The next major issue is that of availability of power. Already we are having shortage of power supply in India. The impending massive prospective growth, which government hopes to achieve in secondary and tertiary sector, to reach a growth rate of 10% annum will increase the demand for power. Then, how can we have power for the massive proposed growth in primary sector, by universally using drip/sprinkler systems, which cannot function without power? The answer lies in universal usage of non-conventional energy for power. Is it available? Let us examine this question.

Feasibility of Non-conventional Power Availability

One major question which comes up as already mentioned for universalising use of drip and sprinkler for irrigation is the non-availability of power. From conventional sources as matters stand there are no prospects of the conventional power, being available in such a massive manner as required by the proposal of universal installation of drip/sprinkler systems in India. However, certain studies, carried out by the Agricultural Finance Consultants as given in the following paragraphs below gives us the hope of required power to run the drip and sprinkler systems.

Power required for drip irrigation schemes for community irrigation wells in Tamil Nadu to lift water are as given hereunder.

Table 12
Requirement of power for using drip system under various crops in Kamarajar District Tamil Nadu

Model No.	Details of area/crop/units of power per day and number of days	Annual Units consumed
Model I	2.4 hectare coconut requires 6.3 units of power for 300 days	1,860
Model II	1.8 hectare guava requires 5 units of power for 300 days	1,500
Model III	2.2 hectare vegetables require 6.2 units of power for 300 days	1,860
Model IV	4.0 hectare mango requires 2.0 units for 250 days	5,000
Model IV A	4.0 hectare acid lime with coconut requires 20 units for 250 days	5,000
Total	14.4 hectare of various crops require	15,220

Per hectare = 15,220/14.4 = 1,056.96 or 1,057 units per annum per hectare generally for 20 metre depth of the well.
(Vide Drip Irrigation Schemes for Community Wells in Tamil Nadu a Feasibility Report prepared for the Government of Tamil Nadu by Agricultural Finance Consultants Ltd. Bombay, August 1989 (vide Appendix 5)

Thus, for different crops with different crop intensity, the requirement of power as in Tamil Nadu, which is situated in the heart of Deccan peninsula where more water is needed for irrigation due to high temperature and climate of the region is presented above. The average requirement of power for lifting from wells and supplying to plants through drips per hectare per annum is given as 1,057 units per annum. Whereas, in the Indo-Gangetic plains, water is traced at a much higher level. Further, in case of surface water delivery from sources of major medium or minor irrigation, there is no question of lifting water against gravity. Water is only taken in such cases and pumped to a place of storage place from where it is further delivered to plants via sprinkler/drips fixed on pipes and it is here that some power is needed. In fact, as we have already discussed, in case of major–medium projects water will reach laterals from where at one cusec flow level water is taken by pumps to a storage tank or elevated tanks by pipes from where water is distributed via pipes to sprinklers and drips fixed on pipes for supply to plants. Further, the ultimate irrigation potential of 140 million hectares is made up of 76 million hectares from surface water and 64 million hectares from groundwater (vide inter-basin transfer proposals, Task Force on Interlinking of Rivers, MOWR, GOI-2003). Therefore, we would not be much incorrect if we assume that, on an average for groundwater we take as an all India average 1,000 units per hectare and for surface water 500 units per hectare because we will be generally simply pushing water without giving much scope for force of gravity to operate. Let us presume this, as our norm for the whole of India because we have seen that in a difficult state like Tamil Nadu drawing water from wells takes 1,057 units per hectare annually for fruits and vegetables which consume more water. Actually, there are foodgrain crops like maize, jowar, wheat that require lesser quantity of water to grow and hence lesser power. But by using drip, even sugarcane we have seen requires much lower quantity of water and hence lower power. Thus, taking 1,000 units per hectare as the norm of power required for groundwater and 500 units per hectare as the norm required for surface water as a representative average for the whole of India for various types of crops, then the power requirement will be 76 million hectares of surface water x 500 units of power + 64 million hectares of groundwater x 1,000 units of power = 1,02,000 million units of power or 1.02 lakh million unit per annum. This will be our demand for power for running drip and sprinkler systems in India universally. Further, 70 million hectares will be area sown more than once. Dividing 70 million hectares in the ratio of surface water: groundwater = 76 : 64 we will have 70 x 76/140 = 38 million hectares from surface water and 70 x 64/140 = 32 million hectares from groundwater. Then, the additional power requirement will be 38 x 500 + 32 x 1,000 = 19,000 + 32,000 = 51,000 million units or 0.51 lakh million units. Thus, total requirement of power will be 1.02 + 0.51 lakh million unit = 1.53 lakh million units per annum.

Energy from Cows – Cowdung

According to an article 'Cows are for ever' by Arun Firodia published in *The Times of India*, 8 December 2004 (vide Appendix 6) the following points emerge.

1. We have the world's largest livestock population, 250 million livestock which produce 125 million tonnes of cow dung per annum.
2. Gobar gas research station in Uttar Pradesh has established that one cow gives enough cow dung in a year to produce 225 litres of petrol in energy terms (or methane).
3. The calorific value table shows that one kg of methane gas is more or less equal in energy content to one kg of petrol, LPG or diesel.
4. According to Arun Firodia, 40 million cows produce energy equivalent of 8 million tonnes of petrol. In other words, 40 million cows produce, 8,000 million kgs of petrol. Further, Arun Firodia has assumed on the basis of findings of Gobar Gas Research Station of Uttar Pradesh that one cow produces, methane equivalent of 225 litres of petrol. Therefore, 40 million cows produce 225 x 40 million = 9,000 million litres of petrol.
5. It is also stated in the article that 200 grams of petrol produce 1 kwh of electrical energy in a generator, or 1 unit of power.
6. Therefore, 1 kg of petrol produces 5 units of electric energy or 1.125 litres of petrol produces 5 units of energy. Therefore, one cow which produces from its cow dung 225 litres methane or equivalent of petrol will produce 225 x 5/1.125 = 1,000 units of electrical energy per annum.
7. There are 250 million livestock annually can produce 250 million x 1,000 units = 2.50 lakh million units of energy which will be more than the requirement of 1.53 lakh million units of energy required annually for operating drips and sprinklers throughout India for irrigating the estimated 210 million hectares of gross irrigated area. Actually, 61% of the 250 million cows or 155 million cows are enough to run our drip/sprinkler sets. In addition, to such a big asset, energy can be generated from other non-conventional sources also which are described later. In addition biogas making produces, bio-manure in the shape of slurry obtained from gobar gas. 50% of cow dung used for producing biogas. This quantity of manure will be as under, i.e., 155 million cows produce 77.5 million tonnes of gobar, which is used to produce 1.53 lakh unit of energy further half of 77.5 million tonnes of gobar will be 38. 75 million tonnes of organic manure will be available as bye-product!

Obtaining methane gas from cow dung is a simple process. A gobar gas plant consists of airtight tank filled with raw organic waste generally cow dung. The anaerobic decay of this matter generates gobar gas. This gas, which is collected in inverted drum has 68% methane, 31% carbon dioxide. If it is passed through limewater carbon dioxide is removed and if it is further passed through iron filings then, the balance of HOS will be removed. The gas then becomes rich in methane and this enriched methane is fed to the generator to produce electricity.

The installation of biogas plants attached with devices for securing enriched methane, which could be fed to a generator, that can generate electrical energy, can be installed in villages by private entrepreneurs who should collect the cowdung on payment basis and in turn produce and sell this energy to farmers for running their drips and sprinklers. It needs to be stated that, as of now, massive usage of biogas for production and supply of power is not undertaken on a commercial scale. Here and there some pilot projects, based on government or community efforts, are organised to produce gas to run *chulas* or for some domestic lighting. In brief, so far no serious attention has been paid to produce and use biogas for generating power. Therefore, totally new initiative involving private enterprise in a massive manner will have to be undertaken. In its wake, millions of jobs will be created.

Wood Gasifier

Wood Gasifier is another method from which electricity can be generated. Cultivable or culturable wastelands (i.e. cultivable lands which have been left as waste for more than five years) were 13.8 million hectares in 1999–2000. Of these 13.8 million hectares, if 6 million hectares could be planted with hard variety of wood like *Prosopis Juliflora* (Bellary Jali), *Glaricidia*, etc., then power could be generated from such plantations. These varieties of wood plants produce 4 tonnes of wood per year in one hectare. Therefore, we can produce 36 million tonnes of biomass for generating electrical energy from 6 million hectares of cultivable wastelands. 7.2 million tonnes of wood or 1/5th of 36 million tonnes can be harvested each year and planted with new plants so that, 1/5th of the area can come up with new trees in the harvested area in the course of five years after harvest. Thereby, we can have continuous supply of 7.2 million tonnes of hardwood per annum for generating electricity.

The potential of wood gasifier can be assessed from the following fact.

1.3 kg of wood can generate 1 kwh or 1 unit of electricity. Thus 7.2 million tonnes or 7200 million kg can generate 7,200/1.3 = 5,538 million units of energy. If in addition to hardwood agricultural wastes like hard tur stalk, cotton stalks, mulberry stalks, paddy husk and groundnut shell pellets are used instead of wood, then, there is a potential of turning the estimated 5,538 million units of power into 8,000 million units of power per annum. Further, the added tree cover will be an advantage for improving the environment and increase in groundwater tables and prevention of soil erosion along with prevention of silt flow to the valleys.

Energy from Bio-diesel

According to Arun Firodia, (vide Appendix 6), the West has already started generating bio-diesel in a big way. Even in India, trees like, pungon, neem, karianji, ratangyot or jetropha can be grown to produce oil. A thousand such trees can be planted in one hectare which yields 10 tonnes of oil seeds, from which 2.5 tonnes of oil can be extracted from one hectare. This oil can be converted into bio-diesel after trans-esterification and used as fuel in diesel engines which can generate electricity. We have seen in Appendix 6 that Arun Firodia has stated that 200 gm of petrol can generate 1 kwh of electricity from a generator, i.e. 1 kg of petrol can generate 5 kwh of electricity. He also stated that, calorific value of petrol, diesel, and methane is the same. Even if 200 gm of bio-diesel are used in the generator 1 kwh or 1 unit of electricity can be generated. Then, 2.5 tonnes of oil or 2,500 kgs of bio-diesel which one hectare can generate 2500 x 5 = 12,500 units of energy. If the 4 million hectares of cultivable wasteland out of 13.8 million hectares (of which we have reserved 6 million hectares for wood gasifier as stated earlier in this report), are used for growing bio-diesel species, then we will have 4 million hectares x 12,500 units = 50,000 million units of energy. Thus, this is another source of non-conventional energy. There is also scope to grow bio-diesel producing species of trees in cultivable land as well as in fallows. Thus, the scope is terrific. Further, trees will add to the much required forest cover in India.

Needless to say, there are other non-conventional methods of generating energy like the wind energy, tidal energy, solar energy, etc., which will provide us adequate non-conventional energy to run our sprinkler and drip systems to be used universally for irrigation in India.

9

Water Budget

There are various estimates of water resources in quantitative terms for the country as a whole. These are taken from the 'Eleventh FYP 2007-12, Planning Commission, GOI and are given below:

TABLE 13 A
Estimates of Water Resources in India

Agency	Estimate in BCM	Deviation from 1869 BCM
First Irrigation Commission (1902–03)	1,443	–23%
Dr A.N. Khosla (1949)	1,673	–10%
Central Water and Power Commission (1954–66)	1,881	+0.6%
National Commission on Agriculture	1,850	–1%
Central Water Commission (1988)	1,880	+0.6%

As seen from Table 13A these estimates differ from each other. However, one more estimate available to us which has been given by Shri Suresh P. Prabhu's 'Task Force Report on Interlinking of Rivers, Ministry of Water Resources, 2003, Inter-basin Water Transfer Proposals'. According to these proposals full justification has been given for the availability of water resources annually in India. The same are given in the following paragraph sub-titled Supply of Water.

Supply of Water

Annual precipitation including snowfall in the country has been 4,000 BCM for centuries and will continue to remain the same for many more centuries to come barring radical climatic change. Groundwater is a part of surface water which percolates into ground. At places, the same groundwater re-appears as surface water through springs or by artificial pumping. Part of the water so pumped again returns to ground after application for irrigation and other uses. The water entering into ground, sometimes percolates into deep aquifers and/or mixes with low quality underground water and saline strata rendering it unsuitable or uneconomical for re-use. Surface water, right from the stage it falls as rain till it finally drains into sea is subjected to percolation and evaporation. The hydrological cycle is thus complex, but final outcome is that out of annual precipitation of 4,000 BCM, 1,869.35 BCM is all that is available as fresh water rest of which is lost in evaporation, percolation or escapes into sea during floods. To the extent we can store this flood water, we can augment lean season supplies. This is possible through large storages. The present availability of utilisable surface and groundwater is at 1,122 BCM (Source: Proposals of Task Force on inter-linking of rivers).

The renewable fresh water resource of India as we have seen is 1869.35 billion cubic metres; Or, 4% of earths water resources and much of this fresh water flows through the Ganga (525.02 BCM) and Brahmaputra along with Barak (585.60 BCM) or a total of 1,110.62 BCM flow through the above mentioned rivers. While all other rivers in India flow 1869.35–1110.62 = 758.73 BCM. Thus, for optimal usage of water inter-basin transfer is necessary by creating storages. With the present in basin utilisation the renewable resources of water is as we have seen 1,122 BCM of which 432 BCM per year is from groundwater. For purposes of this book we will consider 1,122 BCM as the supply of water per annum.

Demand for Water

Different demand scenarios up to the year AD 2050 have been enumerated 'in the Report of the Standing Committee for Assessment of Availability and Requirement of Water for diverse uses in the country' headed by member WP & P, Central Water Commission (MOWR) August 2000. The demand projected for different years is given here under.

Table 13
Demand of Water for Various Sectors

Sector	Water demand BCM in the year					
	2010	% to total	2025	% to total	2050	% to total
Irrigation	688	84.60	910	83.26	1072	74.08
Drinking including livestock	56	7	73	6.68	102	7.05
Industrial	12	1.4	23	2.10	63	4.36
Energy	5	0.6	15	1.37	130	8.98
Others	52	6.4	72	6.59	80	5.53
Total	813	100	1093	100	1447	100

(Extracted from Task Force Report on Interlinking of Inter-basin Rivers)

The above figures of demand in terms of BCM are the same as those given in 'Eleventh FYP 2007-12, Planning Commission, GOI'. The Planning Commission has also cited Ministry of Water Resources as the source of these figures. However, the Planning Commission has given another set of figures for the same years citing National Commission on Integrated Water Resources Development as the source. For purposes of this study we will consider only the Ministry of Water Resources figures which are given in Table 13.

The demand projections include reasonable demand management through larger productivity in irrigated agriculture, more efficient water management (no specific mention of universal use of drip/sprinkler irrigation is made in preparing the above demand scenario, since we have not yet succeeded in bringing sufficient areas under these systems). With presently utilisable surface water of 690 BCM and 432 BCM of annual replenishable groundwater, the total utilisable water available works out to 1,122 BCM, which is sufficient to meet the demand by AD 2025 as seen from Table 13. However, there will be gap between water availability and requirement by 2050 when the population of the country is expected to stabilise at 1,640 million.

Other Demand Scenarios for Irrigation

In Karnataka

Consequent to Krishna Water Disputes Tribunal's (KWDT) award in 1976, a master plan could be drawn up for the Krishna basin area, for utilising 734 TMC of water allocated to Karnataka by the KWDT. This is called scheme 'A' allocation, based on which total irrigation potential under major, medium and minor projects using surface water is planned to be 41 lakh hectare. (Vide Revenue Reforms Commission First Report Volume 1, November 2003).

Based on this, the following working sheet for a year's requirement of water is derived:

1. 41 lakh hectares require 734 TMC of water.
2. or 4.1 million hectare require 734 TMC water.
3. 1 million hectare require 734/4.1 = 179.02 TMC of water.

We know that, 1 cubic metre is = 35. 31 cubic feet.
Therefore, 179.02/35.31 = 5.07 TM cubic metres of water.
But, 1,000 million = 1 billion
Therefore, 1 million hectare requires 5.07 or 5.1 BCM of water.
Therefore, 1 hectare requires 5.1 BCM/1 million = 5,100 Cubic metres.

Case 2

A study called 'Drip Irrigation Scheme for Community Wells in Tamil Nadu – A feasibility Report prepared for Government of Tamil Nadu by Agricultural Finance Consultants Ltd. Bombay, August 1989 brings out the following:

One district, viz., Kamarajar District, has been taken up to be presented here from the above study. The following five models indicate the requirement of water for different crops:

Table 14
Water Requirements

Model	Area/Crop	Litres
Model I	2.1 hectares of coconut requires	1,18,80,000
Model II	1.8 hectares of guava with coconut borders requires	90,00,000
Model III	2.2 hectares of vegetables require	1,18,80,000
Model IV	4 hectares of mango/acid lime with coconut on borders requires	2,38,50,000
Model IV A	4 hectares of acid lime with coconut on borders requires	1,59,00,000
Total	14.4 hectares requires	7,25,10,000

(Vide Appendix 5)

Thus, 14.4 hectares require per annum 7,25,10,000 litres of water. We also know that 1 cubic metre is=1,177 litres.

Therefore, 14.4 hectares requires 7,25,10,000/1,177 61,606 cubic metres of water.

Therefore, 1 hectare requires 61,606/14.4=4,278 cubic metres.

It must be remembered that this requirement of water has come up when drip systems have been deployed. We have assumed earlier in this report that there will be 50% of water savings if drip is used compared with conventional method of irrigation. Therefore, if we add 50% to 4,278 it will be ½ x 4,278 = 2,139; therefore, 4,278 + 2,139 = 6,417 cubic metres per hectare, will be required for conventional method of irrigation for fruits and vegetables.

Thus, from the above studies, we have seen that in the case of Krishna basin the requirement of water is 5,100 cubic metres per hectare, if water is used by conventional method of irrigation for largely protective irrigation requiring low duties (quantities) of water. In Case 2, we have estimated that water requirement per hectare, if conventional method is used is 6,417 cubic metres.

We know that in India, in the North, alluvial soils are there and the climate also remains for a large part of the year considerable cool and rainfall is more and soil moisture regime is high due to number of rivers and the water tables are also very high. There are also areas in the East and North-East and West and North-West, where heavy rainfall occurs and soil moisture is very high due to the riverine nature of the terrain. If soil moisture is more, requirement of water in such areas will also be lower.

Therefore, various regions will require various amounts of water to grow various crops in various seasons. In view of the consumption of water indicated in difficult Deccan plateau terrain, where rainfall is also not high, we can conservatively take the requirement as 6,500 cubic metres per hectare or 6.5 BCM for 1 million hectare for India as a whole on an average.

We have seen that the ultimate irrigation potential of India with present conventional methods of irrigation will be 140 million hectares and the water which will be required at the rate of 6.5 BCM per million hectare will be 140 x 6.5 = 910 BCM without use of sprinkler/drip. But, with this quantity of water if we can universally use sprinkler and drip systems which save 50% of water we will be able to irrigate an additional area equal to 50% of 140 million hectares or on the whole 140+70 = 210 million hectares of gross irrigation. As we have already discussed we will be having a net sown area of 150 million hectares, thereby the 910 BCM of water will irrigate 150 million hectares net sown area and 60 million hectares of area sown more than once totalling to 210 million hectare of gross cropped area. This according to our objective has to happen before 2020.

We know from what is stated earlier in this report that 1,122 BCM is the fresh water available for use in the present largely intra-basin utilisation of water. Therefore, 1,122–910 = 212 BCM of water will be available for other purposes other than agriculture, even with the present largely intra-basin utilisation of water. It may be seen from Table 13, that the Task Force has estimated for AD 2025 1,093 as total requirement of water and 910 BCM for irrigation and thus their estimates for purposes other than irrigation is 1093-910 = 183 BCM. Therefore, availability of 212 BCM in 2020 itself, for purposes other than irrigation will be abundant supply of water exceeding beyond needs of 2025 five years earlier. By inter-linking inter-basin rivers, say, by 2050 another 35 million hectares can be irrigated as per Task Force proposal. Since by 2020 itself we are reaching 210 million hectares of gross irrigation potential, this extra quantity which can irrigate 35 million hectares as and when it becomes available also can be used for other purposes than irrigation to make India strong in water availability. Therefore, the excess water that will become available which, even if we take 6.5 BCM as quantity required per million hectares for irrigation will be 35 x 6.5 = 225.5 BCM which will be available for other purposes. Thus, total of 212 + 225. 5 = 437.5 BCM will be available for other purposes by 2050. Thus, India will be in a very strong position both in production of foodgrains as well as other crops for local consumption and export. Further, availability of water more specifically for drinking and industry, etc., will be also abundant. Needless to say, the Task Force had assessed the demand for non-irrigation needs as 183 BCM in 2025 and 375 BCM in 2050. These assessments of the Task Force will be surpassed if we use drip and sprinkler systems by 2020 itself, provided, we succeed in bringing about utilisation of our ultimate water potential by universal use of sprinklers and drips.

10

Supplemental Sources of Water Supply

Watershed Management

The catchment areas of reservoirs, tanks, streams, rivers are watersheds. When rain falls water flows from ridge lines of each hill or upland down to the plains and into tanks, reservoirs, streams and rivers which we term as valleys. The land from the ridgeline of hills and uplands to the valley is called watershed or catchment area of the valleys. By now in India watershed development which involves protection of soil, preservation of water and extension of tree cover is an established concept and excellent work is being done in this behalf in some places. Since on hills and uplands tree cover has almost been denuded, water flows with silt with great speed only to silt the tanks, rivers, reservoirs, etc., also leading to overflow of the very feeder channels of several water bodies as well as rivers. In order to prevent this, the denuded hilltops should be brought back to have full coverage of trees. These hill tops and denuded uplands have lost so much of silt and become so barren, that in the first year soil binders like growing grass should be applied and thereafter bush type of crop could be taken and only then planting of tree crops is possible. A further method of protecting soil is contour bunding along the contours in all the cultivable fields. This will protect both fertile soil and increase capacity of holding of water in the soil. In addition, *in-situ* conservation of water should be undertaken by constructing farm ponds in the farms and blocking water flowing bodies like brookes, stream or a feeder channel by putting check dams at various points all along their course till they join the valley. This will prevent both flow of silt and promote stoppage of water at various places (of course, allowing excess water to flow without silt to valleys), in order to promote moisture conservation in adjoining lands. Thus, we will have in the cultivable field protected rich soil as well as extended moisture regime which will require lesser per unit water for irrigation. Further, farm ponds, in which rain water is harvested and also gully checks or check dams in the streams, brooks, feeder channels will retain water after rain, thereby extending moisture regime and also giving scope for supplementary avocations like fisheries. Thus, in order to supplement water and improve the fertility and moisture regime of the soil and preventing water sources like tanks, reservoirs, rivers getting silted up, Watershed Management should be undertaken universally in the country. Already a well designed watershed plan is under implementation in the country, but this has to be speeded up to cover the entire country as early as possible. This can be undertaken under funds from the NREGS and rural employment-oriented schemes of GOI, funds from river valley catchment treatment programmes, in addition to funds specifically earmarked for watershed programmes from GOI, state governments and externally aided funds. It needs to be noted that watershed development is a highly employment-oriented scheme in the construction stage and it will also provide continuing benefits to the landless, if in common lands where trees are grown, tree pattas are given to poor families of about 100 trees per family to take care of the same and secure income therefrom by selling the usufruct. In the farm ponds, fisheries can also be practised at least in the rainy seasons along with utilising the farm pond water for irrigation.

Recycling of Water

The water from the gutters and polluted water which comes out from various sources can be treated in water treatment plants and recycled for industrial and non-drinking water needs. This will be a supplement to the water availability in India.

Other Sources

In course of time desalination plants located across our coastline as well as in saline areas will be able to supply fresh water, useful for various purposes including drinking.

The above three sources will supplement effectively our efforts to make the country strong to meet its water supply needs.

11

Cost Estimates of Utilising Irrigation Potential with Sprinkler/Drip

If the entire irrigation potential (net) is to be identified from both surface water and groundwater sources, then we will have to identify the area where potential is created and utilised, where potential is created but not utilised, where potential is utilised but lost due to salination, alkalinity and waterlogging and in case of groundwater the potential created and utilised has to be further bifurcated according to sources with IP sets and without sets in use, etc. All this has been accounted for and is available in Tables 3D and 3E, which gives figures for irrigation adopting FMI. But, we have stated earlier that, since we will deploy universally SMI and DMI methods to irrigate lands we will be able to save 50% of water and hence, 140 million hectares of ultimate irrigated area as assessed now by using FMI systems will increase by 50% of 140 million or we can irrigate 140+70 = 210 million hectares. As a matter of land use policy, we have also stated earlier that 150 million hectares will be the net sown area. Therefore, we will have 150 million hectares of net irrigated area and 60 million hectares of area sown more than once so that the gross irrigated will be 210 million hectares. But, we know that ultimate irrigation potential using FMI method of irrigation is 140 million hectares net, which is made up of 76 million hectares of net sown area under surface water and 64 million hectares under groundwater. Thus, if the net irrigation potential becomes 150 million hectares instead of 140 million hectares, it will mean 10 million hectare of net extra irrigation potential which has to be divided between surface water and groundwater irrigation in the ratio of 76:64. If we so divide 10 million hectares in that ratio, we will have 5.43 million hectares of surface water irrigation and 4.57 million hectares of groundwater irrigation. Therefore, the total net ultimate irrigated surface area will be 76+5.43 = 81.43 million hectares and groundwater 64+4.57 = 68.57 million hectares, totalling to 150 million hectares. From Table 3D we know that 140 million hectares is the ultimate irrigation potential and also that 16.27 million hectares of surface irrigation potential and 24.41 million hectares of groundwater potential had been not created till the end of March 2005. Obviously, if the revised net ultimate irrigation potential is taken as 150 million hectares, then the net irrigation potential for surface water not created will be 16.27+5.43 = 21.70 million hectares and the net groundwater potential not created will be 24.41+4.57 = 28.98 million hectares as at the end of March 2005.

Therefore, in Table 15 below, for items noted in column 2 the area in column 3 has been taken from Table 3D except for area where irrigation potential is yet to be created (vide I b & II b), for which figures worked out above have been incorporated. The unit cost noted for various items in Table 15 below, is taken from Appendix 7.

Table 15
Estimates of the cost of utilising ultimate irrigation potential by 2020 deploying DMI and SMI methods of irrigation

SI No.	Item	Area (million hectare)	Cost per hectare (Rs)	Total cost (Rs Million)
1	2	3	4	5
I	Surface water			
a.	Where irrigation potential is created and utilised			
i.	Lands free from salinity/waterlogging	30.05	43,800	13,16,190

Table contd...

ii	Lands with salinity and waterlogging	14.25	52,800	7,52,400
iii	Total (i+ii)	44.30		20,68,590
b.	Where irrigation potential is created but not yet utilised	15.43	51,300	7,91,559
c.	Where irrigation potential is yet to be created	21.70	2,33,800	50,73,460
D	Total I (a iii+b+c)	81.43		79,33,609
II	Groundwater			
A	Where irrigation potential is created and utilised			
i	With IP sets installed	12.69	38,500	48,88,565
ii	Without IP sets	26.90	80,500	21,65,450
iii	Total II a (i+ii)	39.59		70,54,015
b.	Where irrigation potential is yet to be created	28.98	1,09,000	31,58,820
C	Total II a (iii+b)	68.57		1,02,12,835
III	Grand Total (Id+IIc)	150.00		1,81,46,444

Thus, the total cost of creating infrastructure of universal drip/sprinkler in 150 million hectares net will be Rs 1,81,46,444 or Rs 1,82,00,000 million Rs 18.20 lakh crore. With availability of water, which we have seen, the infrastructure we will create for covering net area of 150 million hectares will obviously cover gross area of 210 million hectares.

Table 16
Cost including repairs

Sl No	Item	Cost (Rs Crore)
1.	Cost of utilising 150 million hectares net and 210 million hectares gross (vide Table 15)	18,20,000
2.	One time repair of distributaries/laterals before they are handed over to DLC and waterusers societies, respectively, for maintenance under major medium projects	160 *

Table contd...

3.	One time repair of minor irrigation works before they are handed over to tankusers societies	670 **
4.	**Total cost**	**18,20830**
5.	**Government expenditure in the above**	
	a. Creating surface irrigation potential of 21.70 million hectares @ Rs 1,82,500 per hectare	3,96,025.00
	b. Reclamation of lands affected by salination/water logging @ Rs 11,500 per hectare for 14.25 million hectare	16,387.50
	c. One time repair of distributaries/laterals of major medium irrigation works and all minor irrigation works before handing over for maintenance to DLC, WUS, etc., (160+670 = 830)	830.00
	d. **Total (a+b+c)**	**4,13,242.50**
6.	**Institutional finance** (item 4 – item 5c)	**14,07,587.50**

Unit cost in item 5a and 5b are taken from Appendix 7

* Every year funds are allocated for repairing Major Medium irrigation projects, therefore a notional amount has been provided for one time repair of distributaries/laterals.
** In the absence of any rational data about repairs, a substantial amount has been provided for one time repair of MI works before they are transferred to tankusers/waterusers societies.

Note: Before handing over these works to waterusers societies, DLCs or tankusers society's onetime repair should be carried out by the government.

As the above Table 16 indicates, 23% is government investment, while financial institutions can fund 77%. It means Rs 4.13 lakh crore will be government investment and Rs 14.07 lakh crore will be the share of financial institutions totalling to Rs 18.20 lakh crore as the overall cost. But, we have seen earlier that total utilisable water both from surface and groundwater sources available to us is 1,122 BCM per annum. As we know from above we will be using 910 BCM to irrigate 210 million hectares of gross cropped areas (150 million hectares net). Therefore, another 1,122-910 = 212 BCM of water will be available for other than agricultural use. Thus, we have to have estimate of cost for harnessing these 212 BCM of water, which will be available for non-agricultural purposes, since, what we have given above relates to cost of water to be supplied for agriculture. For non-agricultural purpose also largely piped network will be used at many places to supply drinking water, etc., we have therefore, presumed that the unit cost of harnessing water will be same as that for agriculture. The cost of harnessing and supply of 910 BCM of water for agriculture, we have seen works out to Rs 18.20 crore. Then, on pro-rata basis the cost of utilising 212 BCM of water for non-agricultural purposes will be Rs 4.24 lakh crore. Even if we take 25% as the government share, since for non-agricultural purposes generally recovery of cost of investment on projects is considered, then government share will be 1.06 lakh crore and institutional share will be Rs 3.18 lakh crore. Thus, insofar as, water requirements are concerned, India will be abundantly surplus in water for carrying out all required agricultural and non-agricultural needs. The total investment required will be Rs 22.44 lakh crore of which the government share will be Rs 5.19 lakh crore and institutional finance will be Rs 17.25 lakh crore.

12

Implementation

In order to implement a massive programme of change over from existing conventional method of flow or flood irrigation to total coverage under drip/sprinkler methods of irrigation, massive efforts are called for. These efforts should not merely be confined to government but should also involve active participation of people: agricultural/horticultural scientists and extension workers/soil scientists, industry and social scientists. Obviously, there should be effective coordination of activities of all concerned, which will contribute to success of such a huge programme.

Government will have to launch a 'Water Mission' with headquarters in Delhi and branches at state/union territory headquarters. As far as GOI is concerned, the Ministry of Water Resources should be the nodal ministry servicing the mission, but the mission proper could be headed by a reputed personality either from science and technology or bureaucracy or public life, provided they are suitable to manage a mission of this magnitude. At the state/union territory level, the mission should be headed by the development commissioner of the respective state or union territory since inter-disciplinary coordination between irrigation, agriculture/horticulture, watershed department, geology department, cooperation department, financial institutions and industries department is called for. But the mission could be serviced by the department of irrigation (water resources in the respective state/UT secretariat).

The mission in each state/UT should prepare an action plan for each major/medium and minor surface water irrigation projects including groundwater projects.

Surface Water

1. In lands where water is already being utilised we have to instal the sprinkler/drip sets. In such lands if the drainage system and on farm development is weak, the same should be made strong so that scope for salinity/alkalinity and waterlogging is avoided.
2. To reclaim the lands, now under salinity and alkalinity and waterlogging by improving drainage systems, on-farm development and applying soil enforcements wherever necessary and carry out installation process of drip and sprinkler systems and reclaim such lands.
3. To expeditiously create irrigation potential which is left uncreated from the sources identified to create the ultimate irrigation potential and utilise it by installing sprinkler/drip systems with a strong drainage system and proper levelling of lands (on farm development).
4. In a, b and c above, due to receipt of water from outlets of laterals of irrigation projects through pipes to be stocked in a storage place in the field before onward delivery by pipes via sprinklers and drip sets to the plants will take place. There will be a minimum saving of 50% of water relative to use of conventional method of irrigation. In order to use the water saved for irrigation due to installation of drip and sprinkler, further extents of land are to be identified and developed to becoming arable under drip/sprinkler irrigation which will be universally installed in such land also.
5. In the process of identifying the extra lands under cultivation, it has to be recalled that we have envisaged the use of current fallow and other fallow lands for cultivation to some extent in addition to net cultivable land. The problems connected with the non-usage of fallow lands should be got reviewed and resolved by the state/UT heads of the mission through deputy commissioners/district collectors/district magistrate and sub-divisional and taluka heads of departments. Chief executive officers of taluk panchayats should also carry out monthly reviews in gram sabhas in which each individual owner/owners of fallow land should be invited. The cultivatorwise and villagewise information

of such reviews should be provided to the district magistrate or DC, who should make use of this and resolve all difficulties to ensure usage of these lands. The voluntary agencies/NGOs duly trained in mass communication methods should be involved to motivate people for bringing such lands into cultivation. Obviously, cultivatorwise and villagewise information should be furnished to such organisation. The inputs for training motivators and NGOs and carrying out mass communication campaigns should come from renowned social science institutes, management institutes and mass communication institutes nearest to the state/UT headquarters.

Groundwater

1. On all existing irrigation wells/bore wells sprinklers/drip sets should be installed. If the yield of such wells is more than what is required for the holding of the owner then he should be legally enjoined upon to sell it to adjoining fields. In fact, the concept of use of irrigation wells/bore wells on community basis should be propagated wherever the holdings of cultivators are small, otherwise if the holdings are big enough, individual wells are recommended. The owner of the land in whose fields the well/borewell is located, should be allowed to collect water charges for supplying water to neighbouring fields in case of community wells. In the Tamil Nadu Community Drip Irrigation Scheme cited in this report, it has been mentioned that a pressure gauge and meter installed at the pipe which receives water from one field to another would indicate the quantum of water used by each field under a well/bore well. At the same time motivational functions devised by social scientists, mass communication experts and implemented by NGOs/government extension staff should create an environment in which everyone takes to drip/sprinkler irrigation.
2. Where new irrigation wells/borewells are drilled in any holdings optimum use of water should be made individually if the holding is adequately large and if not it should be collectively used by the holder of the well/borewell and adjoining land holders with rights given to the owners/wells to collect charges for water supply to neighbours.

Note: it should be noted that this report has assessed that every field will get water if we utilise our ultimate irrigation potential of both surface water and groundwater.

Social Engineering

These massive efforts to succeed require massive management operations which will involve cooperation and coordination among innumerable irrigators. This should be brought about by NGOs/voluntary organisations with their motivators and mass communicators and also through government extension staff. The inputs for securing such cooperation, coordination among people should be provided to the motivators/mass communicators/ extension workers by reputed institutes of social sciences, management institutes and mass communication institutes nearest to the state or UT headquarters. This work also should be coordinated by the development commissioner through deputy commissioners, district collector/district magistrates, Chief Executive Officer (CEOs) of zilla panchayat concerned.

Agriculture and Horticulture

Massive support to the cultivators of 210 million hectares of gross area should be provided by agricultural and horticultural scientists/soil scientists (to test soils of each field), through the extension machinery of the department of agriculture and horticulture, seed producing/selling agencies, research scientists to formulate and implement farm plans by using the willing cooperation of the cultivators. Here also, lot of motivation is called for by involving NGOs. It needs to be noted that the farm plans should have minimum 136 million hectares under foodgrains crops to meet the national food requirements. The most well suited crops for each type of soil both in horticulture and agriculture which will secure maximum returns to the cultivators should be propagated. This calls for training of extension workers, seed producing agencies, mass communicators and NGOs, so that they use this knowledge to bring about optimum benefits from this massive irrigated agriculture. In devising the training programmes the agricultural universities should play a major role.

Manufacturing Industries

The state/UT development commissioners, as heads of the mission at that level should, with the help of industries department play a proactive role to invite private sector, to set up drip, sprinkler and pipe manufacturing units at district headquarters and if required, at more than one place in the districts in a time frame which synchronises with the massive needs of irrigation with universal use of sprinkler and drip systems. Similar action for manufacturing *gobar* gas plants and allied requirements like electrical generators, etc., should be taken. Needless to say, this will lead to unprecedented spread of low tech industries at the district headquarters and the semi-urban/peri-urban areas. As far as training in use of drip/sprinkler systems and their maintenance/repair is concerned the manufacturing industry should be asked to appoint local dealers in their jurisdiction. These dealers should not be merely in-charge of an area to sell the sprinkler/drip sets and ancillary items like pipes, etc., but they should also be made responsible for imparting the training in operation of the drip/sprinkler sets to the farmers and carrying out after sales service and repairs including supply of spare parts. Towards this the dealer should be asked to maintain the workforce of the local youth who have studied up to at least eighth standard and trained by the manufacturers for maintenance. If ITI certificate holders are available in the area they can more profitably be engaged by the dealers with training given to them by the manufacturers. It should be impressed on the dealers that the continuity of the dealership will last as long as they are providing effective after sales service to the farmers. The manufacturers should make their own arrangements to collect feedbacks from the farmers on the after sales performance.

The manufacturers should also be enjoined upon to give preference to local engineering and diploma holders and other skilled or unskilled staff to be inducted in their manufacturing units. In fact, such personnel should be given pre-induction training by the manufacturers. This will lead to a lot of employment opportunities in industries, in areas which hitherto have not had such opportunity of spread of industry.

Processing Industries

The private sector should be encouraged to set up processing industries at district, talukas and even lower levels, to process the increased agricultural produce adding value to the primary product. In fact, contract farming and organised selling nearer villages could be encouraged so as to secure assured market/better price for cultivators. In the processing industries, local technically qualified persons should be preferred for employment. Further, the unskilled labour obviously will come from the same area.

Infrastructure

The increased agricultural produce in the rural areas resulting from such a massive irrigation project will need supporting infrastructure of supply of inputs like fertilisers, seeds, roads, warehouses (including refrigerated ones) and markets which should be adequately strengthened and expanded, preferably by greater participation of the private sector. The state heads of mission should appropriately plan and implement the same.

Mission at Headquarters of India

The mission at the headquarters (New Delhi) should annually, meet before the commencement of the year, help the state missions in formulating the projects for the year and monitor the performance and provide all counselling the state missions to make the programme a time-bound success.

e-governance

The entire operation shall have to be executed deploying e-governance tools. In fact, if the village level database of survey numberwise details indicating its present irrigational status is fed to the computer, it could provide information we need to carryout the irrigational inputs which are enumerated in this report. In addition, if the nature of soil after carrying out soil test takes the shape of a survey numberwise database it would be of tremendous help in planning for propagation of proper crops particularly as irrigation becomes available to each survey number. Further, the spread of installation of sprinkler and drips with accessories along with spread of irrigation can be monitored survey numberwise. It is needless to mention that several benefits from grass root level monitoring supported by appropriate outputs to help the district, state and country level administration to follow up implementation of this programme will accrue. In the maintenance stage also it would be of tremendous help.

Benefits from Implementation

The benefits from the implementation of this programme are numerous. Some of them are counted here under:

1. The net cultivable land will increase from present 143 to 145 million hectares to 150 million hectares giving a big boost to the national income from the primary sector, particularly if we consider that 150 million hectares of net irrigation will become 210 million hectare of gross irrigated area consisting of 60 million hectares of area sown more than once. Further, by universal use of drip/sprinkler water will be supplied in a regulated manner to the crop according to the needs of their growth thereby leading to increase in quantity and quality of produce. Further, the cost of cultivation will be reduced because operations like de-weeding will be minimal. Availability of 38.75 million tonnes of gobar slurry from gobar gas plants will help organic plant cultivation substantially. Therefore, the returns to the individual cultivators will be substantial. The nation will be in a strong position not only to feed 1,640 million people, at which India's population will stabilise in the year 2050, but even the cash crops/non-food crop production will increase beyond our needs. This will make India a big exporter of foodgrains fruits and vegetables and processed products, cotton oil seeds, etc.
2. The spread of sprinkler and drip manufacturing industry in district/taluka headquarters will give considerable employment not only to the qualified engineers but also to the skilled/semi-skilled people at village level leading to increased national income in secondary and tertiary sector.
3. The food, fruit, oil seed, cotton, etc., processing units which are programmed to be located at district, talukas and lower levels have their own employment benefits for the qualified engineers/the educated workforce/skilled, semi-skilled people. The farmers are assured for the sale of their produce at appropriate prices, if contract farming with the processing units is brought about in a big way.
4. With so much of greenery around and availability of feed and fodder, the animal husbandry sector will also thrive.

5. The large number of engineers we are producing in India every year will find ample employment opportunity with higher incomes, nearer to their homes since the emphasis is in locating industries in dispersed even in rural areas.
6. A number of new entrepreneurs in the shape of manufacturers/distributors/dealers would get scope for high employment opportunities to enterprising educated people to take to these industries/dealership, etc.
7. The expansion of infrastructure of roads, market yards, godowns, banks, railways will also take place leading to further creation of employment opportunities in areas which have been deprived of the same except in metros and bigger cities.
8. The need for expansion and extension of our airports and development of hitherto, undeveloped harbours will also arise in order to meet the greater export needs of produce from primary sector. Actually reporting in *The Times of India* dated 20 April 2006 under the title 'Farm products' export may be the 'next big thing'. Mr Darlington Jose Hector for TNN, has stated that the next move over in the country is from IT/ITES to the farmer/the milkman. India's peaches, mangoes and oranges too could make its way to US and European markets in next three to five years. Indian cereals, soups and milk derivates like butter and cheese or other products that are waiting to knock on international doors. Given the potential, the Centre has decided to invest $ 22 billion over the next eight years in processing and packaging of fruits, vegetables and other agricultural products. Corporates like Reliance, ITC and Bharti are entering the sector. Bharti has set up Field Fresh Foods, a 50-50 JV with the Rothschild Group, for this venture. Its plan is to export apples, litchis, cherries, tomatoes, baby corn and lettuce sourced through the contract farming route to Europe, UK, South East and west Asia. Wal-Mart has said, it is working towards sourcing basmati rice, tea, shrimps and spices from India. Germany's Metro Group sources cardamom, pepper and honey from here. An official in Metro said agri-product sourcing will be the 'next big thing' in India. 'Metro plans to source commodities such as basmati rice as also fruits and vegetables. We may even do fish to supply to East Asian markets,' he said.
9. More than anything else, increased agricultural produce will gradually demand mechanised agriculture, even if it is required to be used on a

community basis because many of the holdings are small. The small farmers/farm labourers should be given functional literacy if they are literate, coupled with training in operation of mechanised tools equipments, etc. In fact, even those who are illiterate can be trained to use and maintain such machinery, since all these are low tech areas. Obviously, this will give rise to the need for another industry for manufacturing mechanised agricultural tools/equipments/machinery to be again located at district, taluk and lower levels. It is needless to mention its impact on employment in secondary and tertiary sectors including repairs.

10. Needless to say, with spread of so much prosperity in rural areas resulting from irrigation and industry the incomes of people are bound to rise. With increasing incomes, better participation of children in schools and affording of better health facilities will be available. In fact, in the rural areas the social security insurance product assuring the community of education and health expenses would succeed, since capacity to pay for premium will be there with the people. That is, we will be providing urban incomes in rural areas.
11. Last but not the least, we will utilise our non-conventional sources of energy to the optimum extent. As a bi-product of this, organic manure in the shape of slurry coming out of biogas plants will be available in quantities never before made available to the cultivators.

Thus, this project will be a blue print for eradication of unemployment, poverty, illiteracy, ill health and spell in its wake rise of incomes in areas which are away from the islands of prosperity, with congestion we have created in our metros and other big cities. Further, with increasing incomes along with health, education and habitat development will also take place. People will build better houses with increased incomes. In addition, needless to say, India will become a big agricultural force. In brief this project will bring about the much talked of second agricultural revolution coupled with social and economic betterment of the people.

South African Water Policy

In Appendix 8, we have presented a 'White Paper on South African Water Policy'. This indicates how water use policies during apartheid regime were helping the whites to use water for agricultural purposes depriving other South Africans of water even for essential needs like drinking and sanitation. It also brings out the need of water for industry, etc., which has to come up to provide jobs to all south Africans. The paper, tries to solve these problems through legislative means which will judiciously distribute water and recommends for such a law. However, we have commented that in addition to legislative means, South Africa can even deploy micro hydel systems substantially to economically use water and thereby, achieve considerably the objective of their proposed legislation for equitable distribution of water among all the claimants, if they have not done so.

Appendix 1

Illustrations of India's irrigation marvels

Recorded evidence of the use of water finds mention in Kautilya's *Arthashastra*, who was the mentor of Chandragupta Maurya (321 BC). In the chapter entitled 'Heads of the Department (HoD)' he says of irrigation head as under:

'He should build (Irrigation supply) with natural water resources or for water to be brought from elsewhere. To others who are building these he should render aid with land, roads, trees (to reduce evaporation losses) and implements and also give aid to holy places and parts. If one does not participate in the joint building of an irrigation work, his labourers and bullocks should be made to do his share of work and he should share the expenses, but will not receive any benefits from it.'[1] What a concept of participation between government and responsible people designated for a job! In these days, having spent crores of rupees and failed to utilise even the massive irrigation potential created by government, we are crying hoarse about people's participation and experimenting with water users's societies to take care of at least management of distribution in the twenty-first century AD. That is over 2000 years later!

In the *Arthashastra*, in another chapter judges, Kautilya lays down that 'in case of damage to the ploughing or seeds in another's field by the use of a reservoir channels or field under water, they shall pay compensation in accordance with the damage.'[2] Today, we have World Bank lecturing to us on the need for just relief and rehabilitation measures for families affected by irrigation works. We listen to it since we are borrowers.

In another chapter entitled, 'Non-observance of conventions' Kautilya observed among other things that 'if one obstructs a customary water course we use or makes a new one that is not customary, the lowest fine for violation

---

[1]State of India's Environment – a Citizens Report-4 – Dying Wisdom Rise, fall and potential of India's traditional harvest system by Centre for Science and Environment p.11

[2]Ibid p.11

shall be imposed.'[3] Actually in those days the fine was not payment of fine but rectification of causes, which led to the fine. Today, we know that over 40% of the planned ayacut in Tungabhadra project left bank canal in Karnataka is not receiving water due to selfishness of cultivators in the upper reaches of the canal. These upper reach cultivators flagrantly violate the government direction to use prescribed quantity of water, which entitles them to grow only semi-dry crops like jowar, groundnut, cotton, etc., but instead they grow heavy water consuming crops like rice and sugarcane and apparently do injustice to tail-end users who never receive water and hold almost 40% of the land in the command area. How our age-old wisdom and sense of justice has evaporated from us! We are blinded by greed. How wisely Gandhiji had said that India has everything that is required to meet our needs and certainly cannot provide for our greed!

In Indian historic records or rock edicts, declaration of kings who ruled this country till the advent of the British are replete with orders where the people who benefit from irrigation fully participated in either construction or maintenance and even both. People's participation at times of need for repair of irrigation was obligatory, either they had to participate or provide labour in lieu of their absence in certain cases. There were varied systems of people's participation at different times in different areas of India, but whatever be the system they did participate to keep the life lines of water supply of the nation alive.

Two instances of indigenous irrigation systems which existed in the country before the arrival of the British and which were unwittingly destroyed by them due to their sheer inability to understand the usefulness of the same are given below.

Bihar

'The Ganga flows through Bihar. The Himalayan Rivers Ghaghra, Gandok, and Kosi among others which flow through North Bihar to join the Ganga keeps North Bihar fertile as Uttar Pradesh.

But in South Bihar, which lies between Chota Nagpur plateau and the Ganges the terrain has low water retaining capacity. Here, the groundwater level is very low and digging wells is very difficult except in areas adjacent to the Ganga. In Southern bank of the Ganga, a number of swift flowing rivers, viz., the Son, Ponpun, Morhar, Mohane and Gamani are main tributaries of Ganga which start from the plateau and flow down to the Ganga. This slope

---

[3]Ibid p.11

of South Bihar plateau is roughly at the rate of one metre per kilometre from plateau downwards. Therefore, the rivers flow very swift up to Ganga. In order to serve the dual purpose of saving the lands from floods and also to make use of the water for purposes of irrigation, South Bihar had evolved an indigenous unique system of irrigation called the pyne and ahar system. Using the sloppy terrain of South Bihar, an ahar, was built by erecting an embankment of a metre or two in height. From the extreme ends of these embankments, two other embankments were constructed to project towards the higher ground. These gradually reduce in height as the ground level rose and ultimately ending at ground level where water could be found. An ahar thus resembled a rectangular catchment basin with embankments on three sides. Unlike tanks, the beds of the ahars were not dug out. Ahars are sometimes built at the end of small rivulets or artificial channels like pynes to ensure water supply. Obviously, the water in ahars with sides that were more than one kilometre long, irrigating more than 400 hectares were not rare; those smaller ones were more common. Though tanks did exist but they were of minor importance.

Pynes were channels constructed to utilise water from rivers/rivulets flowing through hilly terrains intersecting the country. In South Bihar rivers were generally dry for most of the year, but swell during monsoon season. Given the slope and sandy soil, the water is either carried away rapidly or it percolates down through the sand. Hence, a system of pynes was usually developed to lead water from the rivers to agricultural fields. Some of the biggest pynes, which were over 20-30 kilometres long, fed a number of distributaries and irrigated over 100 villages. They also supplied water to ahars wherever such ahars were constructed to receive water from pynes.

Since beds of sandy rivers were high, the pynes were not dug very deep. Given the scope, they facilitated irrigation within a short distant from their origin. To raise water level in the pynes, they were temporarily blocked at suitable lengths. In some cases, pynes were impounded at the tail end to store excess water. Alternately, small pynes led off from ahars for distribution and such ahars received water directly from rivulets. Both ahars and pynes carried water and supplemented and complemented each other during rainy seasons from July to September, and acted as reservoir against untimely or scanty rainfall.

Nirmal Sen Gupta, who analysed the system, writes although apparently crude, the ahar-pyne system, is a remarkable indigenous system making possibly the best out of natural conditions. Apart from irrigation facilities, there is another utility of the system. Being a region between Chota Nagpur plateau and Gangetic valley, South Bihar is very prone to floods, but the abundance of storage works like ahars and large scale dispersion of torrential flood waters into pynes minimised the rush and speed of flood waters passing through South Bihar. Some of the small rivers could never reach the Ganga or the Punpun because their water was completely dispersed through several pynes.

The responsibility of constructing ahars and pynes lay mainly with zamindars of South Bihar. The expenses, both for constructing and repairing these works were entirely defrayed by the zamindars. Besides, there was a collective system called Goam, in which every cultivator had to supply one person per plough to carry out physical work. But zamindars fixed the date of Gaom. Thus, it was people's participation which suited those zamindari days. The zamindars after mid-September, when water supply became less, used to allocate water to different tenants under their zamindaris while at other times, when pynes were full, any tenant could draw any quantity of water. Each village has fixed quota for number of days or hours of water as per this system, which was called 'Parabandi', the system worked on the basis of a register called 'Lalbahi', which was maintained with zamindars, specifying rights of villages.

So long as zamindari revenues were collected by zamindars in terms of share of produce, this system worked excellently as long as produce rent system remained in force, the zamindars benefited from the construction and upkeep of irrigation works, they were quiet willing to fulfil their responsibilities under the zamindari system.

Reportedly, the return on capital investments in irrigation works secured by the zamindars was 40% to 50% in the first year and in some cases as much as 100% under produce rent system. As long as the produce rent remained in force and the zamindars were to benefit from the construction and upkeep of irrigation works, they were quit willing to fulfil their responsibilities. Under zamindari system the indigenous irrigation system in South Bihar was blessed by the decentralised management with zamindars or their functionaries acting as irrigation leaders.

When the British came to power in the nineteenth century, a provision was made under Bengal Tenancy Act (1885), Bengal then included Bihar, for allowing commutation of produce rent to fixed cash rent, restrictions were imposed on indiscriminate use of systems in complicated areas. In a year when largescale commutation was allowed the irrigation system almost collapsed over large parts of South Bihar. The increase in areas of cash rent coincided to a large extent with the decline of the irrigation system in the district of Gaya wrote collector of Gaya in 1938. He also wrote that a great deal of distrust in Gaya district is due entirely to the decline of production of land and only to a lesser degree due to fall in prices, even though it was a year of depression. I have visited a large number of 'Nagdi' (Cash rent) villages and the conditions of these villages is deplorable. It is obvious that nothing has been spent on 'Gilandasi' (improvement of irrigation works), since commutation took place. The story was repeated throughout South Bihar.

The reason is that produce rent is just not land rent; it is a rent on another variable, viz., irrigation in addition to land. In South Bihar with limited technology of extending scope for irrigation, land does not have an identity separate from irrigation. Produce is the result of land plus water. Obviously, produce rent is more efficient. The zamindar would take interest in maintaining the irrigation systems in such a case.

Once cash rents were fixed and zamindars had nothing to lose from the decline in irrigation, they stopped taking care of those works. In addition they started irrigation works, as a lever of control – by cutting off irrigation supplies, they forced many tenants to produce less and abandon their holdings in rent default which were then settled by the zamindars with new tenants with cash rent levy at higher rates. Unscrupulous zamindars rented out the silted ahar belts for cultivation. At first, this was done on the pretext that it was only for rabi crops grown during those months when ahars do not contain water. But soon the same belts came under paddy cultivation.

Another reason was that the zamindaris were divided and sub-divided as time passed by. So, where earlier one pyne was under one zamindar, it came to be owned by many. Attempts made rather successfully in the early stages to establish cooperation among the zamindars for coordinated repair. A headman, viz., zamindar who owned largest number of villages made an estimate of cost of repair and apportioned it among others proportionately. The others contributed the amount allotted to them and work was finished under the supervision of the headman. But such cooperation became more and more difficult as the zamindars engaged more and more in litigation. In case a zamindar was disinclined to carry part of his job the coordinator had no powers to compel him to do so. The Bihar – Orissa Private Irrigation Act 1922 was the law which recognised this unwillingness as a legal offence and the Act empowered the district collector to become the irrigation leader in such disputed cases. But for seventeen more years when it was amended in 1939, the Act was practically of no use. The collector was required to serve several notices to unwilling proprietors to 'satisfy' himself that they were unwilling to take up those tasks. Several years would elapse in tedious preliminaries before the actual work could begin. All this time the irrigation works deteriorated further, a few went beyond repair. For those which could be repaired, the collector could not spend more than Rs 2 per acre to recover the cost incurred from the treasury for such repair works, within a time limit set. No irrigation works could be repaired within that limit.

Another reason for considerable damage of the system of irrigation was that, if due care was not taken in the construction or repair of the pynes, the river would alter its course and make the pyne its new course. The original path of the river would then get silted up and the irrigation arrangements down the original course would be rendered useless, while villages along new course would suffer floods.

All that can be said is that the indigenous systems took care of proportion of efforts by landlords and tenants in the matter of irrigation by a psychological recognisation of the benefits each would secure. The political chaos and demoralisation of people, whether landlords or tenants, which came about due to British regime which enacted laws that did not take into account socio-economic realities; resulted in these disasters. Because it is said that, research may reveal the contribution of the system rendered to the extension of settlements of South Bihar. Even the shifting of the ancient capital from the highlands of Rajagriha to flood site of Pataliputra was related to success achieved at that time in controlling floods through the network of ahars and pynes.

Now, the systems are being rehabilitated slowly. The two evidences are the Gram Bharathi Sarvodaya Ashram of Jamui District which helped 45 Bhoodan beneficiary families owning 100 acres to offer Shramadhan and realise the benefit of an ahar. Similar revival of ahar andpyne systems was done in Khaspur in Nobadpur. These have been revived with government help in the 1990s. These are healthy signs, but too little efforts are being made. We must re-dig our traditional wealth, wherever we can with speed and political will to do so.'[4]

Bengal Irrigation

'In Bengal, the system of overflow irrigation was very popular. It consisted of long canals parallel to each other. Irrigation function was performed by

---

[4]State of India's Environment – a Citizens Report – 4 – Dying Wisdom Rise, Fall and Potential of India's traditional harvest system by Centre for Science and Environment - Summarised from p. 86 to 93.

cuts made in banks of rivers, which allowed water to flow through the canals along with fine silt and supplied water to every field along with enrichment of its soil.

According to Sir William Willcocks, a British irrigation expert who had also worked in Egypt and Iraq and had delivered a series of lectures in the 1920s 'the delta of Ganges is not a rainless area. It enjoys rainfall of about 50 to 60 inches. At that time all the rivers are in flood and to make use of the Ganges and the Damodar floods and the abundant nutritionally poor water of rainfall that some early king put in practice the system of overflow irrigation of the Damodar and Ganges deltas ensured health and wealth to Bengal for hundreds of years. This system is perfectly suited to the needs of Bengal'. He added that the inundation parallel canals were in vogue in the region till about two centuries ago. Flood waters entered through the parallel inundation canals supplied not only rich silts with water but also fish which swam through the canals into lakes and tanks to feed on the larvae of mosquitoes. This helped check malaria in the region. Willcocks observed that, although monsoon between June and October never failed in Bengal and in fact it is heavy, but it may end early. If rain water alone irrigated rice fields they will cry out for irrigation in October because river water availability is poor in October as the monsoon has ended early. If however, the farmer uses rainwater together with flood water in early months of monsoon when the river water is rich and full of mud the crop is fortified enough to resist the hard conditions of an early passing out of the monsoon. The flooding of rivers begins with the same monsoon rainfall which prepares the soil for the sowing or planting of rice. And, as the rains advance, the dry and barren plains become damp and they get covered with water and the mosquito larvae begin to breed in millions. It is just then the muddy waters of rivers come down with millions of eggs of the finest crap, inferior fish and shrimps into canals from rivers. Guided by the banks of the canals and the water courses, the fish eggs went everywhere and soon all the canals and water courses were full of fish. The fields and water tanks also became full of fish which ate the mosquito larvae. Thus, the overflow irrigation combated malaria, provided an abundant harvest of fish, enriched the soil and made congestion or siltation of rivers impossible. Willcocks observed, 'unaided by flood irrigation it impoverished the soil and cannot combat malaria' Willcocks was impressed when paddy crops stand in rainwater and rivers gets flooded, 'the overflowing turbid water of rivers (through canals) often blessed the country as they mingled with the rain waters in the fields and manured it .It also helped to eliminate malaria mosquito and thus combating malaria in the region.'

Needless to mention, the deltas of Ganges and Damodar had a number of small rivers by means of which the deltas are formed and Bengal is known for its many small rivers in addition to the major ones mentioned above. From all these rivers canals were taken distinguishing features of which according to Willcocks were:

- The canals were broad, shallow, carrying crest waters of the river floods rich in fine clay and free from coarse sand.
- The canals were long and continuous and fairly parallel to each other and at right distances from each for the purposes of irrigation.
- Irrigation was performed by cuts in the banks of the canals which were closed when the floods was over.
- The procedure of irrigation, according to Willcocks was as follows: Once the engineer breaches the rivers and the water flows in the canals the same was handed over to local boards working through peasantry. They together were expected to see to it that water reached every field. Thus, even in Bengal after water was made available it was the responsibility of the local boards and peasantry to see to it that water reaches every field.

About AD 1660, Bernier visited Bengal twice and wrote about it before the breakup of the Mughal Empire. In one of his works he said 'the knowledge I have acquired of Bengal in two visits inclines me to believe that it is richer than Egypt. It exports in abundance cotton, silk, sugar, rice and butter. It produces wheat, vegetables, grains, etc., for its own consumption. It has immense herds of pigs and flocks of sheep and goats. Fish of every kind it has in profusion from Rajamahal to the sea. It is an endless number of canals cut in from the Ganges by immense labour, for navigation and irrigation, as Indians consider the Ganges water as the best in the world'.

In 1794, after the Maratha Afghan war, a treatise was written by several Englishmen of Calcutta and printed in 1803 and 1806. 'In the tract of annual inundation, insulated habitations and fields raised considerably above the country exhibited the effect of patient industry.' There were dykes to check inundation, reservoir and dams. Irrigation, Bernier found was less neglected. He stated 'In the management of forced rice, dams retain water in extensive plains or preserve it in lakes to water lower lands, as situation may require. For either purpose much skill is exerted in regulating the supplies of water.

Stupendous dykes could not prevent inundation but check sudden excesses. Strategically constructed dams assisted cultivation of considerable tracts. The treatise adds that, reservoirs, watercourses and dykes were in a process of decay rather than a state of improvement.

In 1794, after the Maratha Afghan wars, the irrigation systems were disturbed and the zamindars and tenants had neglected the work of 'Pulbandi' that is, repairing canals and repairing banks. It could have been revived but the British being navigators and traders with no knowledge of irrigation seeing many waterways neglected after the war; thought that these were canals only for navigation. Decay had begun in central Bengal in 1815 and later in Burdwan where canal clearances were neglected. Hence, there remained nothing but filling up breaches made in the banks of Damador as uncleaned canals took less and less water, more water remained in the Damador and it became a menace to the region. The Damodar banks assumed fresh importance. These banks were known as zamindari banks, they were breached by the peasantry when the fear of inundation has passed or a breach had occurred elsewhere. In this way the old canals definitely dead rivers were filled with water and the region was irrigated more or less perfectly and this was called zamindari bank irrigation.

Then came the final blow to overflow irrigation in Bengal. It was imagined that these zamindari banks were only flood protective works and that they were made solely for that purpose. Zamindari bank irrigation when the breaches or Kanwas were made and the canals or Kanas were filled with water was considered by the British as non-existent. The overflow canals were called dead rivers in some cases and 'drainage lines in some other places' but the word irrigation was never used. Irrigation still went on zamindars and tenants made secret breaches in the banks and irrigated their fields. These breaches were considered by the British authorities as breaches made by uncontrolled floods of the rivers and government set itself to put an end to such discreditable occurring. It never seems to have occurred to anybody in the government that the breaches were made secretly by the peasantry for irrigation. But it ought to have been evident that 40-50 breaches in heavily embanked river of inconsiderable length in a single year could not possibly have been made by the river itself. A committee in 1846 recommended that embankments on the Damodar be removed 'breaches that were closed be reopened' and the river allowed to flow freely down the overflow canals, which they called drainage canals. It also recommended the maintenance and clearance of the canals. Nothing, however, was done as the canals were not cleared and the embankments on the Damodar remained! The banks were frequently cut for irrigation (of course, by peasants) but officials declared it as breached. According to the Gazetteer 25 breaches took place in 1847, 14 in 1849, 56 in 1850, 45 in 1852 and 28 in 1854, the government took over the embankments in 1885 and made them water tight. No more wholesale breaches were allowed to take place.

When the government took over the work it thoroughly strengthened the left embankment. The East Indian Railway made a second embankment. The Grand Trunk Road which was always breached in olden times was raised higher and made into a third embankment and the Eden canal with 5 banks like 5 satanic chains, bound the Damodar, and once healthy and prosperous region between it and Hoogly started facing problems of malaria and poverty.

About Burdwan and Hoogly which were deprived of their overflow irrigation, the district gazetteer of Burdwan, says 'Dr French in his special report on the outbreak of epidemic fever estimated the total mortality at about 1/3 of the total population between 1862 and 1872'. According to Willcocks the peasants were also deprived of fish, naturally irrigation was worst effected. No official figures of the nineteenth century are available about irrigation, double cropping, etc., if Willcock's assumptions are correct, compared with more than 8 lakh acres of canal irrigated area in early part of nineteenth century, there were only approximately 1.3 lakh acres in 1911 in 7 districts of Murshidabad, Birbhum, Midnapore, Bankura, Howrah and Hoogly and one other district. The low yields declining cropped area created a state of decadence and stagnation in all spheres of economic activity in rural West Bengal between 1850 and 1880; scarcity was a regular feature in Bengal. In 1880, a Famine Commission was set-up to investigate possibility of creating permanent relief measures. In the twentieth century, poverty manifested itself in distinct fall in crop yields, in the contraction of the area under cultivation and significant depopulation in western and central Bengal. It seemed that nothing less than a famine could shake the complacency of the government. In 1896-97 a severe drought led to a food crisis and a second famine Commission had to be set-up. Two great famines followed immediately in 1897-88 and the other in 1899-1900. It was after such calamities that first Irrigation Commission was set-up in 1901. Its recommendations were implemented only on a moderate scale and had little impact in Bengal. The Royal Commission on Agriculture set-up in 1926 singled out the case of Bengal as unique. But in doing so, it presented a one-sided argument that drainage, not lack of irrigation, was the cause of Bengal's miseries. In fact, it stated that, 'problem in Bengal differs from that of other parts of India; that it arises from too much rather from too little water'. The Commission referred to problems of drainage congestion as a problem caused by choking of the rivers through sedimentation and siltation, etc. In fact, the Commission appears not to have taken note for reasons of sedimentation and siltation, which were caused by embanking of rivers and giving a go-by to flood irrigation systems, which prevented siltation of rivers and brought all-round prosperity through the flood irrigation canals which carried water with silt to the fields along with fish and fish carp to manure soil, and increase water supply along with rain and raise fish everywhere, to eat mosquito larvae. Thus, the Commission appears oblivious of the fact that almost all problems, with which it was so deeply concerned, were inevitable results of obstructing irrigation. It seemed unable to understand that the people of Bengal had been previously managing to cope successfully with the problem of 'too much water' because they had devised a method for redistributing excess water over vast areas and utilising it to their advantage.

This is how prosperous Bengal was made poor Bengal by wrong policies of the British, which supplanted an irrigation system that functioned for centuries successfully, by full involvement of the people'.[5]

[5]State of India's Environment – a Citizens Report – 4 – Dying Wisdom Rise, Fall and Potential of India's traditional harvest system by Centre for Science and Environment - Summarised from p. 93 to 98.

Appendix 2

Mid-Term Appraisal of Tenth Five Year Plan – Major and Medium Irrigation Physical Details (in '000 ha)

M																
Sl. No	Name of State/UT	Ultimate Irrigation Potential	Achievement Up to March'02 (Ninth Plan)		Target for X Plan		Target for AP 2002-03		Achievement 2002-03		Target for AP 2003.04		Anticipated Achievement 2003-04		Target 2004-05	
			PC	PU	PC	PU	PC	PU	PC	PU	PC	PU	PC	PU	PC	PU
1.	Andhra Pradesh	5000.00	3303.22	3051.59	739.88	480.92	133.94	119.56	94.24	61.26	190.20	123.63	46.73	30.37	264.05	171.63
2.	Arunachal Pradesh	0.00	0,00	0.00	4,00	2.60	0.80	0.52	0.80	0.52	0.80	0.52	0.80	0.52	0.80	0.52
3.	Assam	970.00	243.92	174.37	116.10	75.47	26.80	17.42	5.50	3.58	29.15	18.95	29.15	18.95	47.53	30.89
4.	Bihar	5223.50	2680.00	1714.83	948.42	400.00	170.00	110.50	27.00	17.55	223.00	144.95	45.0	29.25	236.00	153.40
5.	Chat-tisgarh	1146.93	922.50	760.74	305.00	198.25	93.00	60.45	58.00	37.70	47.00	30.55	47.00	30.55	47.00	30.55
6.	Goa	62.00	21.17	15.33	26.66	14.69	5.46	3.55	1.72	1.12	5.46	3.55	3.15	2.05	5.69	3.70
7.	Gujarat	3000.00	1430.37	1300.83	1904.00	1237.60	235.00	152.75	144.00	93.60	24.44	30.44	24.44	30.44	24.44	30.44
8.	Haryana	3000.00	2099.49	1849.97	119.00	77.35	41.00	26.65	16.30	10.60	22.76	14.79	13.57	8.82	17.30	11.25
9.	Himachal Pradesh	50,00	13,35	7.51	8.00	5.20	3.00	1.95	0.20	0.13	0.30	0.20	0.30	0.20	0.30	0.20
10.	Jharkhand	1276.50	354.47	230.45	315.00	204.75	54.15	35.20	3.56	2.31	54.15	35.20	4.82	3.13	49.83	32.39
11.	Jammu Kashmir	250.00	179.69	168.75	25.00	16.25	1.40	1.20	1.40	1.20	5.95	3.87	2.98	1.94	7.27	4.73
12.	Karnataka	2500.00	2121.12	1844.82	999.89	649.93	221.29	143.84	57.12	37.13	241.63	157.06	241.63	157.06	241.63	157.06
13.	Kerala	1000.00	609.49	558.87	90,00	58.50	10.00	6.50	10.00	6.50	15.00	9.75	15.00	9.75	15.00	9.75
14.	Madhya Pradesh	4853.07	1386.90	875.63	265.30	127.20	101.75	66.14	101.75	66.14	100.97	65.63	100.97	65.63	52.00	33.80

Sl. No	Name of State/UT	Ultimate Irrigation Potential	Achievement Up to March'02 (Ninth Plan)		Target for X Plan		Target for AP 2002-03		Anticipated Achievement 2002-03		Target for AP 2003.04		Anticipated Achievement 2003-04		Target 2004-05	
			PC	PU	PC	PU	PC	PU	PC	PU	PC	PU	PC	PU	PC	PU
15.	Manipur	135.00	28.15	20.28	28.15	18.30	-	-	-	-	-	-				
16.	Meghalaya	20.00	0.00	0.00		-	-	-	-	-	-	-	-	-		
17.	Misoram	0.00	-	-		-	-	-	-	-	-	-		-		
18.	Nagaland	10.00	0.00	0.00		-	-	-	-	-	-	-	-	-	-	
19.	Orissa	3600.00	1826,56	1794.17	465.07	302.30	23.22	15.09	29.92	19.45	64.93	42.20	67.40	43.81	44.21	28.74
20.	Punjab	3000,00	2542.48	2485.99	160.30	104.20	Nil	Nil	2.19	5.03	26.09	16.96	Nil	Nil	26.09	16.96
21.	Raiasthan	2750.00	2482.15	2313.87	413.80	268.97	49.30	32.05	44.80	29.12	52.00	33.80	68.85	44.75	87.00	56.55
22.	Sikkim	20.00	0,00	000	0.00	0.00	0.00-	-			-		-	-		-
23.	Tamil Nadu	1500,00	1549.31	1549.29	9.38	6.10	0.84	0.55	4.25	2.76	5.14	3.34	5.14	3.34	5.14	3.34
24.	Tripura	100,00	4,90	4.50	10.50	6.83	-	-	-		2.89	1.88	2.89	1.88	2.4	1.56
25.	Uttar Pradesh	12154. 00	7910.09	6334.00	1000.76	650.49	145.34	94.47	145.34	94.47	158.00	102.70	158.00	102.70	158.00	102.70
26.	Uttaranchal	346,00	280,30	185.41	6.20	4.03	1.24	0.81	1.24	0.81	4.50	2.93	4.50	2.93	4.50	2.93
27.	West Bengal	2300,00	1683.29	1527.12	700.00	455.00	65.00	42.25	39.00	25.35	20.00	13.00	7.52	4.89	15.00	9.75
28.	Union Territories	98.00	6.51	3.94	0.00	0.00	0.00	0.00	0.00	0.00	0.00	0.00	0.00	0.00	0.0u	0.00
	Total	58465.00	36918.43	30919.50	9936.84	6194.59	1502.53	976.93	812.33	513.91	1344.36	888.39	1004.84	667.70	1551.18	1022.82

Appendix 2 Contd.

Mid-Term Appraisal of Tenth Five Year Plan – Minor Irrigation Physical Details (in '000 ha)

Sl. No	Name of State/UT	Ultimate Irrigation Potential	Achievement Up to March'02 (Ninth Plan)		Target for X Plan		Target for AP 2002-03		Anticipated Achievement 2002-03		Target for AP 2003.04		Anticipated Achievement 2003-04		Target 2004-05	
			PC	PU	PC	PU	PC	PU	PC	PU	PC	PU	PC	PU	PC	PU
1.	Andhra Pradesh	6260.00	3019.46	2781,22	195.40	156,32	11,70	9,36	7,23	5,78	16,18	12,94	10,33	8,26	27,13	21,704
2.	Arunachal Pradesh	168,OO	99,52	77.40	20,00	16,00	4,13	3,30	4,13	3,30	4,13	3,30	4,13	3,30	4,13	3,30
3.	Assam	1900.00	603,62	494,11	116,10	92,88	26,80	21.44	14,00	11,20	3,94	3,15	2,25	1,8	6,35	5,08
4.	Bihar	5663,50	4716.44	3759.46	264,60	211,68	52,92	42,34	42,34	33,87	5292	42,34	42,34	33,87	52,92	4234
5.	Chat-tisgarh	571.00	487,70	322,86	55,00	44,00	20,00	16,00	29,10	23.28	38,00	30.40	38,00	30.40	38,00	30.40
6.	Goa	54.00	19,14	20,00	4,54	1,86	0,22	0,18	0,33	0,26	0,33	0,26	0,38	0,304	0,65	0,52
7.	Gujarat	3103.00	1998,92	1876,14	64,00	45,00	6,50	5,20	6,50	5,20	6,50	5,20	6,50	5,20	6,5	52
8.	Haryana	1512.00	163095	1578,12	42,50	34,00	8,50	6,80	6,72	538	8,50	6,80	Nil	Nil	Nil	Nil
9.	Himachal Pradesh	303.00	161,00	138,30	10.00	8,00	2,09	1,67	2,09	1,67	2,00	1,60	2,00	1,60	2,00	1,60
10.	Jharkhand	1183.50	588,87	471.09	56,93	45,54	18,64	14,91	1,74	1,39	19,32	15.46	6,15	4,92	11,215	897
11.	Jammu Kashmir	1108.00	382.45	366,77	23,50	18,80	1.40	1.12	1.40	0,90	523	4,18	3,36	2,69	6,25	5,00
12.	Karnataka	3474.00	1585.40	1541,74	221,29	177.03	8,00	6.40	8,00	6.40	800	6.40	8,00	6.40	8,00	6.40
13.	Kerala	1679.00	640,02	603,76	50,00	40,00	7,00	5,60	7,00	5,60	10,00	8,00	10.00	8,00	10,00	8,00
14.	Madhya Pradesh	11361.00	2256,13	2149.48	125,00	100,00	35,00	28,00	35,00	28,00	30,00	24,00	30,00	24,00	25,00	20,00

Sl. No	Name of State/UT	Ultimate Irrigation Potential	Achievement Up to March'02 (Ninth Plan)		Target for X Plan		Target for AP 2002-03		Anticipated Achievement 2002-03		Target for AP 2003.04		Anticipated Achievement 2003-04		Target 2004-05	
			PC	PU	PC	PU	PC	PU	PC	PU	PC	PU	PC	PU	PC	PU
15.	Manipur	469.00	75.49	62,34	14.45	11.56	3.40	2,72	3.40	2,72	3,30	2,64	3,3	2,64	3,50	2,80
16.	Meghalaya	148.00	50,97	47,31	12,50	10,00	2,97	2,38	2,97	2,38	1,64	1,31	1,64	1,31	188	1,50
17.	Misoram	70.00	16,69	14,08	1,66	1,33	0,23	0.22	0,23	0,22	0,23	0,22	0,23	0,22	0,35	0,30
18.	Nagaland	75.00	76,56	65,63	9.43	7,54	17,92	14,34	Nil	Nil	2,29	1,83	2,29	183	3,60	2,88
19.	Orissa	5293.00	1474,12	1337,55	132.37	105.90	30.37	24.30	30.37	24.30	20.56	16.45	20.56	16.452	42.08	33.66
20.	Punjab	2967.00	3427,56	3367,82	Not fixed	Not fixed	4,37	3.50	2,34	0,24	1,08	0,86	0,18	0,02	1,08	086
21.	Raiasthan	237800	2447,10	2361,80	50,00	40,00	7,00	5,60	4,00	3,20	2,00	1,60	1,8	1.44	5,00	4,00
22.	Sikkim	50.00	29,67	23,61	5,00	4,00	0,50	0.40	0.40	0,32	0.80	0,60	0,80	0,60	0,80	0,60
23.	Tamil Nadu	4032.00	2123,38	2119,52	9,02	7,22	4.46	357	068	0,54	5,21	4,17	5,21	4.17	5,21	4,17
24.	Tripura	181.00	109,65	9609	32.40	25,92	7,30	5.84	7,30	5,84	7,06	5,65	6,05	4.84	6.47	5,18
25.	Uttar Pradesh	17481.00	21599.40	17279,62	3616,80	2893.44	375.43	300,34	373,92	299,14	368,32	294,66	368,32	294,66	368,32	294,66
26.	Uttaran-chal	518.00	500,98	400,80	11,88	9,50	2,38	1,90	2.38	1.90	2,38	1,90	2,38	1,90	2,38	1,90
27.	West Bengal	4618.00	3792,52	3098,12	500,00	400,00	100,00	80,00	65.00	52,00	7000	56,00	70	56	75	60
	Total States	81382.00	56856.31	49012.46	6802.37	5433.92	820.23	656.22	685.57	546.64	709.92	567.93	693.50	554.67	743.82	595.03
	Union Ter-ritories															
28.	A&N Islands		1.38	1.35	0.81	0.65	0.16	0.13	0.16	0.13	0,16	0,13	0.16	0.13	0.16	013
29.	Chan-diqarh		0.26	0.24	0.16	0.13	0.02	0.02	0.02	0,02	0,02	0,02	0.02	0,02	Nil	Nil

Sl. No	Name of State/UT	Ultimate Irrigation Potential	Achievement Up to March'02 (Ninth Plan)		Target for X Plan		Target for AP 2002-03		Anticipated achievement 2002-03		Target for AP 2003-04		Anticipated achievement 2003-04		Target for 2004-05	
			PC	PU	PC	PU	PC	PU	PC	PU	PC	PU	PC	PU	PC	PU
30.	D&N Haveli		0.69	0.65	0.95	0.76	0,19	0.15	0,19	0,15	0,19	0,15	0.19	0,15	0,19	'0.15
31.	Daman& Diu		15.37	10.29	0.96	0.77	0,19	0.15	0.19	0,15	0.19	0,15	0,19	0,15	0,19	0.15
32.	Delhi		21.64	18,52	NF	NF	NF	NF	NF	NF	NF	NF	NF	NF	NF	NF
33.	Lakshad-weep		0.00	0,00	0,00	0.00	0.00	0.00	0,00	0,00	0,00	0,00	0.00	0,00	0.00	0,00
34.	Pon-dicherry		4,37	4,36	2,50	2.00	1.41	1.13	1.41	1,13	1.90	1,52	1,90	1.52	1,85	1.48
	Total (UT"s)	46.00	43.71	35.41	5.38	4.30	1.97	1.58	1.97	1.58	2.46	1.97	2.46	1.97	2.39	1.91
	Total (States &UT's)	81428.00	56900.02	49047.87	6807.75	5438.23	322.20	657.80	687.54	548.22	712.38	569,90	695.96	556.64	746.21	596.94

Note: PC – Potential Created, PU- Potential Utilised

Appendix 3

Development of Minor Irrigation Potential through Plans

million hectares

Plan	Minor Irrigation Total Potential Utilised	Minor Irrigation Groundwater Potential	Percentage of Groundwater to Total Minor Irrigation potential
II FYP	14.75	8.28	56
Annual Plans 1966-69 3 years	19.00	12.50	66
IV FYP 1969-74	23.50	16.44	70
V FYP 1974-78	27.30	19.80	73
Annual Plans 1978-80 2 years	30.00	22.00	73
VI FYP 80-85	35.25	26.24	74
VII FYP 1985-90	43.12	33.15	77
Annual Plans 2 years 1990-92	46.54	36.25	78
VIII FYP	48.80	NA	–
IX 1997-02 anticipated	49.00	NA	–

Source: Ministry of Water Resources and Reports of Working Groups and Tenth FYP proposals for various states.

Appendix 4

Landuse Classification and Irrigated Area in India 1998-99 and 1999-2000 (provisional)

Sl. no.	Landuse type	Area in Th. Ha. 1998-99	Area in Th. Ha. 1999-2000
1	Geographical area	3,28,726 +	
2	Reporting area for land utilisation statistics	3,06,053	3,06,054
3	Forest	68,980	69,024
4	Not available for cultivation		
	a. Area put to non-agricultural uses	22,803	22,967
	b. Barren and unculturable land	19,512	19,440
	Total (a+b)	42,315	42,407
5	Other cultivable land excluding		
	a. Permanent pastures and other grazing lands	11,127	11,040
	b. Land under miscellaneous tree crops and groves not including in net area sown	3,629	3,618
	c. Culturable wasteland	13,904	13,828
	Total (a+b)	28,659	28,486
6	Fallow land		
	a. Fallow lands other than current fallows	9,929	10,108
	b. Current fallows	13,589	14,798
	Total (a+b)	23,518	24,906
7	Net area sown	1,42,581	1,41,231
8	Total cropped area	1,93,034	1,89,740
9	Area shown more than one (8-7)	50,453	48,510
10	Net irrigated area	57,077	57,238
11	Gross irrigated area	75,954	76,336

(MOA, GOI)

Appendix 5

Tamil Nadu Community Drip Irrigation Scheme, Kamarajar District

Model I (2.4 hectares coconut, 6 beneficiaries)
Power:
Motor 4 HP according to area of location from well/depth of water available in summer. 200 LPM/20 metres head at outlet near main line of drip (LPM: Litres Per Minute)
Usage:
Plants in 2.4 hectares with yield 200 LPM for 3.3 hours per day 6.2 units per day for 300 days
Electricity consumed:
6.2 x 300 = 1860 units per annum
Water lifted and consumed:
200 LPM x 60 metres x 3.3 hours x 300 days = 1,18,80,000 litres

Model II
Plants (Guava) 1.8 hectares with coconut borders – 4 beneficiaries
Power:
2.5 HP motor according to area of location to well – depth of water availed in summer, etc., – 200 LPM/20 metres head at outlet.
Usage:
Plants in 11.8 hectares with yield 200 LPM for 2.5 hours per day – 5 units per day for 300 days
Electricity consumption:
5 units x 300 = 1,500 units
Water lifted and consumed:
200 LPM x 2.5 hours x 60 metres x 300 days = 90,00,000 litres

Model III
Plants 2.2 hectares vegetables – 5 beneficiaries
Power:

2.5 HP motor according to area of location to well; depth of water availed in summer, etc., – 200 LPM/20 metres head at outlet.

Usage:

Plants, in 2.2 hectares with yield 200 LPM for 3.3 hours per day – 6.2 units per day for 300 days.

Electricity consumption:

6.2units x 300 = 1,860 units.

Water lifted and consumed:

200 LPM x 3.3 hours x 60 metres x 300 days = 1,18,80,000 litres.

Model IV

Plants 4 hectares mango/acid-lime with coconut border – 10 beneficiaries.

Power:

.5 HP motor according to area of location to well; depth of water availed in summer, etc., – 300 LPM/20 metres head at outlet.

Usage:

Plants in 4 hectares with yield 300 LPM for 5.3 hours per day – 20 units per day for 250 days.

Electricity consumption:

20units x 250 = 5,000 units

Water lifted and consumed:

300 LPM x 5.3 hours x 60 metres x 250 days = 2,38,50,000 litres.

Model IV A

Plants 4 hectares acid-lime with coconut border.

Power:

2.5 HP motor according to area of location to well; depth of water availed in summer, etc., – 200 LPM/20 metres head at outlet.

Usage:

Plants, in 2.5 hectares with yield 200 LPM for 5.3 hours per day – 20 units per day for 250 days

Electricity consumption:

20 units x 1,250 = 5,000 units.

Water lifted and consumed:

200 LPM x 5.3 hours x 60 metres x 250 days = 1,59,00,000 litres.

Abstract

Kamarajar District Power Consumption in the Five Models.

Model	Area Covered hectares	Units of Electricity Consumed Per Annum
I	2.4	1,860
II	1.8	1,500
III	2.2	1,860
IV	4.0	5,000
IVA	4.0	5,000
Total	14.4	15,220

Average power consumed per hectare
15,220/14.4 = 1,056.9 or 1,057 units per annum.

Abstract of water consumption

Model	Area Covered hectares	Water consumed Per Annum (Litres)
I	2.4	1,18,80,000
II	1.8	90,00,000
III	2.2	1,18,80,000
IV	4.0	2,38,50,000
IVA	4.0	1,59,00,000
Total	14.4	72,51,000

1 cubic metre = 1,177 litres

Therefore, per hectare water lifted and consumed = 7,25,10,000/1,177 x 14.4 = 4,278 cubic metre.

(vide drip irrigation schemes for community wells in Tamil Nadu – A Feasibility Report prepared for the Government of Tamil Nadu by Agricultural Finance Consultants (formerly, Agricultural Finance Corporation) Bombay, August 1989.

APPENDIX 6

Cows are Forever, Methane Gas, the Answer to Oil Imports

By Arun Firodia

US President George W Bush recently made a fervent appeal to the developed world to take to methane farming. He rightly said, methane farming would counter the skyrocketing prices of crude oil and emerge as an alterative to fossil fuels whose stocks may be depleted in the next thirty to forty years. Methane farming is nothing but generation of biogas from starch or organic waste such as cowdung. A developing country like India should take up methane farming, in view of our rapidly growing energy requirements.

We have the world's largest livestock population of 250 million which produces close to 125 million tonnes of cowdung. Using this, we can produce enough methane gas to entirely replace LPG and kerosene in cooking, and substitute petrol in transportation. Methane gas can also generate enough electricity to meet all requirements, at least in rural areas. The by-product can serve as excellent organic manure, substituting chemical fertilisers which require LNG as feedstock.

The gobar gas research station in Uttar Pradesh has established that, one cow gives enough cowdung in a year to produce methane gas equivalent to 225 litres of petrol in energy terms. The calorific value table would show that one kg of methane gas is more or less equal in energy content to one kg of petrol, LPG, kerosene or diesel.

LPG is generally used for cooking in urban areas while kerosene is the preferred fuel in rural India. A 15 kg LPG cylinder lasts about two months for a family of six. This works out to 15 kg of LPG per capita per year. The same holds true for kerosene. The entire LPG and kerosene requirements of our 100 crore population can be met by methane gas cylinders, produced from the cowdung of 75 million cows.

Just like CNG, methane gas can be used to run automobile engines in place of petrol. Our petrol consumption last year (2003-04) was eight million tonnes. On the assumption that one cow produces methane gas equivalent to 225 litres of petrol, we will need about 40 million cows to produce an energy equivalent to eight million tonnes of petrol.

A generator needs 200 gm of petrol to produce one kilowatt/hour (kwh) of electrical energy. The per capita electrical energy consumption in rural area is 112 kwh per annum. Our rural population being 74 crore, we will need another 85 million cows to meet the electrical energy needs or rural areas. This comes to a total of 200 million livestock to satisfy our energy requirements.

Obtaining methane gas from cowdung is simple enough. It consists of an airtight tank filled with raw organic waste like cowdung. The anaerobic decay of this matter generates gobar gas. An agitator quickens the process. The gas is collected in an inverted drum. This gas has 68% methane and 31% carbon dioxide. It is passed through lime water to remove the carbon dioxide and over iron fillings to remove HoS. It then becomes enriched with methane.

The gobar gas plants are available in various sizes, from three cubic metres to 270 cubic metres, costing between Rs 20,000 and Rs 1,00,000.

A compressor can extract and compress this methane gas into portable cylinders. These methane gas cylinders can then be used for cooking, or in automobiles and two wheelers. As much as 50% of the cowdung slurry is available as leftover in the gobar gas plant, which then can be used to produce organic manure rich in nitrogen and phosphorus. The cowdung of 200 million cows can produce 50 million tonnes of manure, which can be used for two rotations in a year to take care of the fertiliser needs of the entire 143 million hectares in the country. This will completely offset the need to import LNG, used as feedstock in fertiliser plants.

If every village (of which we have 6.27 lakh) has 50 farmer families who maintain just two bullocks and four cows each, the cowdung of these animals can produce enough methane gas to take care of country's entire energy needs, now being met by LPG, kerosene, petrol and LNG. Besides, this livestock can provide rural electricity as well.

The West has already started generating bio-diesel in a big way. Even in India, trees like pungan, neem, karanji, ratanjyot or jatropha can be grown to produce oil. A thousand such trees can be planted on one hectare, which will yield 10 tonnes of oilseeds, from which 2.5 tonnes of oil can be extracted. This oil can be converted into bio-diesel after esterification and used as fuel in diesel engines. Our annual requirement of diesel oil last year was 38 million tonnes.

This amount of bio-diesel can be produced by trees planted on 15 million hectares of fallow or wastelands. And, we do have 25 million hectares of fallow land. In other words, we can generate enough bio-diesel to meet our entire need of diesel oil.

Methane farming and bio-diesel are the new renewable sources to meet our entire energy needs. Why should we import oil from the Gulf or gas in a pipeline via a hostile Pakistan, when we can manage from our resources?

Source: (*The Times of India,* 8 December 2004)

APPENDIX 7

Cost of Creating and Utilising Irrigation Potential

I. Creating irrigation potential by conventional methods – Surface water. The cost of creating 1 hectare of irrigation potential is Rs 1.25 lakh in 2005 as can be seen from the study. At a 4% rise of cost per annum in 15 years, i.e. by 2020 the cost will compound to

Rs 1,25,000 x $(1+4/100)^{15}$ = Rs 1,25,000 x 1.95 = Rs 2,43,750 or Rs 2,40,000.

The average cost per annum in the period 2005 to 2020 can be taken as average of lowest cost+highest cost

= (1,25,000+2,40,000)/2 = Rs 1,82,500 per hectare.

This will apply for all surface schemes major medium and minor approximately across the board. In any case, as may be seen from Table 3D, only 16.27 million hectares is the potential yet to be utilised for surface irrigation from ultimate 76 million hectares.

II. Utilising irrigation potential created by conventional methods both in surface and groundwater.

To utilise water by conventional method, we have to create FICs to receive water from laterals at 1 cusec level outlet, carry out land levelling called OFD and construct FDCs to drain water from the fields to join the main drainage channel of the area. The water is generally received from laterals of the concerned project at, out of 1 cusec level in surface water schemes, and in case of groundwater it is just pumped by irrigation pump sets from the depths at which water is traced.

In Table 5, the costs for different components for utilisation of water by land development necessary have been worked out and are reproduced as Table A.

Table A
Utilisation of Irrigation Potential – Component wise cost (Command Area Development Works as on March 2003)

Sl No.	Component of work	Area covered in lakh hectares	Cost (Rs Crores)	Cost per hectare (Rs)	Each component as percent of total cost
1	2	3	4	5	6
1.	Field irrigation channels	21.20	1,224.51	5,776	51
2.	Field drainage channels	12.73	96.30	757	7
3.	On farm development works	20.30	926.19	4,740	42
	Total cost per hectare	-	-	11,273	100

(vide report of First Revenue Reforms Commission Vol –I Nov-03 p. 390)

If as on March 2003, the cost of utilising irrigation potential by conventional methods of irrigation is as given above, then the costs of utilising irrigation potential in 2005 at 4% rise in cost per annum is as under for the year 2005:

$11{,}273 \times (1+4/100)^2 = 11{,}273 \times 1.12 = 12{,}626$ or Rs 12,600.

In 2020 the cost will be $12{,}600 \times (1+4/100)^{15} = 12{,}600 \times 1.95 =$ Rs 24,570 or Rs 24,000 for conventional methods of irrigation.

The componentwise cost of utilisation of water in 2005 and 2020 can be had by multiplying the cost of utilisation by percentage of cost of each component as given in column 6 of Table A. The same is worked out and indicated in Table B.

Table B relates to conventional method of irrigation (FMI). But if drip/ sprinkler method of irrigation is used there will be no need of field irrigation channels, since pipes will receive water from laterals of projects at 1 cusec level in case of surface water irrigation and take it to an elevated storage place, from where it is supplied to plants via sprinklers and drips. In case of irrigation pump sets of groundwater it is lifted from well/borewell and supplied via sprinkler or drip sets fixed on pipes to plants. Therefore, in both cases only on farm development can be carried out and field drainage channels can be constructed to drain water spilled out from sprinkles or

Table B
Componentwise cost of development

Sl	Component of work	Cost in 2005	Rs	Cost in 2020	Rs	Average cost of 2005 & 2020	Average Cost in the period 2005–2020 (Rounded off)
1	Field Irrigation Channel	12,600 x 51/100	6426	24,000 x 51/100	12,240	9,333	9,300
2	On Farm Development	12,600 x 42/100	5292	24,000 x 42/100	10,080	7,686	7,700
3	Field Drainage Channel	12,600 x 7/100	882	24,000 x 7/100	1,680	1,281	1,300

leaking water from drip systems or to drain the rain water whenever it rains. Therefore, when changeover to universal drip and sprinkler is taken up, all that will be necessary by way of carrying out utilisation of potential created will be carrying out OFD works and construction of FDCs, i.e. taking up works mentioned at item 2 and 3 as components of work in Table B above. However, it needs to be mentioned that, where irrigation potential created is already being utilised, all that we have to do is to check whether land levelled under OFD is intact and the drainages constructed are surviving. Obviously, where irrigation is being utilised some expenditure will be needed to carry out repairs of OFD and FDC since some repairs will be necessary in these components of work. This applies across the board for all irrigation potential to be utilised whether by surface water major, medium or minor or groundwater utilisation.

III. Average cost per hectare of land development for utilisation of irrigation potential (freshly created) before installing sprinkler/drip

Thus, if new irrigation potential is created and it is to be utilised using sprinkler and drip, the land development required will be consisting of only two components, viz., OFD and FDC. Therefore, the cost per hectare on land development will be as under in the period 2005-2020 on an average per annum vide Table B above.

OFD: Rs 7,700
FDC: Rs 1,300
Total: Rs 9,000 (for surface water)

But in case of groundwater where land development has to be carried out in different places the estimate is taken as Rs 10,000 per hectare.

Average cost per hectare where utilisation is already being carried out during 2005 to 2020 before installing sprinkler/drip – repair of OFD/FDCs

If irrigation potential is being utilised in the conventional way then, all the three components will be there on the field, but still over a period of time they would have been worn out and repairs will be needed. In view of the fact that FICs are no more needed because pipes will be used to deliver water to plants instead of FICs; we can take it that on an average about 1/4th of the cost of OFD and FDCs should suffice to carryout proper repairs and bring these two components on par with newly developed lands, so that fixation of sprinkler/drip and other accessories will make them functional again. Therefore, the cost on land development (OFD+FDC) repairs will be about 1/4th of Rs 9,000 or Rs 2,250 or Rs 2,500 on an average per hectare in the period 2005-2020 and then land development could be followed by fixation of drip/sprinklers and other accessories.

Average cost per hectare of reclaiming land affected by salinity and waterlogging

In respect of lands which have become alkaline or saline or waterlogged, these have to be properly levelled and drainage system set right, i.e. OFDs and FDCs should be proper and alright. In other words, the entire cost of Rs 9,000 per hectare would be required for land development and prevention of future emergence of alkalinity, etc. In addition, about Rs 2,500 could be kept as cost per hectare for application of gypsum, etc., so that soil is treated to bring the land into proper crop yielding condition. Thus, for all such lands Rs 11,500 will be the cost per hectare.

IV. Surfacewater utilisation through sprinkler/drip installation

A case study entitled 'Feasibility Report for Comprehensive Landuse Management Project for Harkanhal Mandal – Bellary District, Karnataka conducted by M/s Agricultural Finance Consultants Limited; January 1989 is cited hereunder to secure the costs for utilising irrigation potential created by using sprinkler and drip (other than land development cost).

Study of a minor irrigation tank in Harkanahal Mandal by deploying sprinkler systems

1. Village: Togarikatte, Harkanahal Mandal, Bellary District
2. Source of water: Minor irrigation tank.
3. Present command of the tank: 20 hectares by flow irrigation method.
4. Designed area using sprinkler.
   Sprinkler – 50 hectares for protective irrigation, i.e. 1 hectare becomes 2.5 hectares or 150% increase over the present capacity for protective irrigation. Heavy duty crops are cultivated under irrigation, we have assumed 50% increase in the area. However, as may be seen later in this case study 2.5 hectares of protective irrigation become 1.5 hectare of heavy duty irrigation. Therefore, the ratio of cost between protective irrigation and heavy irrigation will be 2.5: 1.5 or 2.5/1.5.Therefore, for purposes of calculating costs of installing sprinkler and drip we will take 1.5 as the norm for heavy irrigation against 1 hectare without use of sprinkler and 2.5 hectares with irrigation but with protective irrigation.
5. Cost estimates

Table C
Cost of installing of sprinkler system

Sl No.	Item	Cost in (Rs)
1.	Cost of 14 sprinklers with pipes and accessories	1,51,400
2.	Cost of 75 HP electric motor with accessories	1,23,700
3.	Civil works construction of storage tank of capacity 420 M^3 (12M x 10M x3.5M) along with one pump house (7.5 M x 3.5 M with AC sheet)	79,200
4.	Electrification deposit with electricity boards	21,500
5.	Miscellaneous charges	37,600
	Total cost	4,13,400

Note: In case we use drip irrigation the cost of using the same will be more or less what is given above. Thus, in this study we will take the same cost per hectare for both sprinkler and drip.

Derivations from Table C:

a. 50 hectares of protective irrigation requires Rs 4,13,400.
b. Therefore, for 1 hectare = 4,13,400/50 = Rs 8,268.
c. Then, for heavy irrigation, the cost will be 8,268 x 2.5/1.5 = Rs 13,780. or Rs 13,800 per hectare. This was the cost in 1989.
   Then, cost in 2005 will be 13,800 $(1+4/100)^{16}$ = 13,800 x 2.03 = Rs 28,014 or Rs 28,000.
   Then, the cost in 2020 will be 28,000 x $(1+4/100)^{15}$ = 28,000 x 1.95 = Rs 54,600.
d. The average cost between 2005 and 2020 will be (28,000+54,600) /2 = Rs 41,300.

Cost where irrigation potential is yet to be created.

Table D

Actual cost per hectare of irrigation under sprinkler and drip where irrigation potential is to be created and utilised (surface water)

New irrigation potential is created the cost will be as under:

Sl No.	Item	Cost in (Rs) per hectare	Source
1.	Cost of creating irrigation potential	1,82,500	Para I
2.	Land development		Para II
a.	On farm development	7,700	
b.	Constructing drainage channels	1,300	
3.	Cost of motor/sprinklers/drips with accessories and construction of storage tanks	41,300	Note d. below Table C
	Total	2,33,800	

6 A. Cost where irrigation potential surface water, is created but not yet utilised

In Table D above item 2 and 3, i.e. the cost of land development plus cost of motors, sprinklers and drips is to be taken and this works out to Rs 50,300 per hectare.

Cost per hectare where irrigation potential is being utilised by conventional methods (FMI)

In case water is already being utilised and sprinkler/drip and motor, etc., with accessories is to be installed, then, the only difference in cost will be that of land development (OFD+FDC), i.e. repairs of OFD and FDCs are carried out. That is the cost will reduce be as under:

1.	Repair of OFD and FDC	Rs 2,500
2.	Cost of motor/sprinklers/drips with accessories and construction of storage tanks	Rs 41,300
3.	Total cost pre hectare (1+2)	Rs 43,800

Cost per hectare where irrigated land is affected by salinity/ waterlogging

In case of land reclamation the cost per hectare will be as under:

1.	Cost of land development with land treatment, etc.	Rs 11,500
2.	Cost of motor/sprinklers/drips with accessories and construction of storage tanks	Rs 41,300
3.	Total cost per hectare (1+2)	Rs 52,800

IV. Groundwater creation and utilisation of irrigation potential Case Study of Harkanhal Mandal

A. Cost of Borewell

1.	Borewell	Rs per unit
a.	Cost of drilling borewell 152 mm diameter bore hole down to a depth of 50 metres @ Rs 190 per metre	9,500
	If all India norm of 30 metre depth is at Rs 190 per metre it will cost	5,700
2.	Cost of 150 mm inner diameter electro resistance welded casing pipe @ Rs 230 per metre (length of casing pipe the thickness of weathered mantle encountered while drilling normally it varies from 15 metres to 20 metres for estimating unit cost 19 metres is assumed though in certain regions it may be lesser)	4,465

3. Yield test charges with submersible pump for 6 – 8 hours (lump sum)	500
4. Geo-physical investigation charges for locating the site for drilling the borewell (lump sum)	400
5. Transport of equipment (lump sum)	250
6 a. Total cost with 50 metre depth borewell (1a+2+3+4+5)	15,115 or 15,100
6 b. Total cost with 30 metre depth borewell (1b+2+3+4+5)	11,315
B. **Motor and accessories**	
1. Cost of submersible 3 hp motor pumpset	12,000
2. Accessories inclusive of control panel, G-valves energisation charges, installation charges, miscellaneous.	10,500
Total	**22,500**
C. Cost of sprinkler set installation	17,400
D. Cost of drip set installation	21,500

Source: Comprehensive Landuse Management Project - A Feasibility study - Harkanhal Mandal by Agricultural Finance Consultants, Bombay 1989.

Note: The cost of drilling a borewell will be more or less equal to digging an open well to the corresponding depth by building a parapet wall on it. Therefore, the above costs can be taken to apply to an open well also.

The above costs will create 1.6 hectares of irrigation.

The borewell or dug well constructed with the above cost will be capable of irrigating with sprinkler/drip, 1.6 hectares of area under heavy duty crops as we have seen in the case of community irrigation well study in Tamil Nadu although more area can be covered under heavy duty crop.

Working sheet for cost per hectare

Sl No.	Item	Costs for 1.6 hectare (Rs)	Cost per hectare (Rs)
1.	Drilling borewell with accessories/digging an open well with parapet walls up to 30 metres depth	11,300	7,063
2.	Motor and accessories	22,500	14,062
3a	Cost of sprinkler installation on borewell/dug well	17,400	10,875
3b	Cost of drip installation on borewell	21,500	13,437
4	Total cost of borewell with motor+sprinkler installation	51,200	32,000
4 a	Total cost of borewell with motor+drip installation	55,300	34,562

Assuming that half the groundwater area will be under drip and the other half under sprinkler irrigation, the average cost per hectare will be:

32,000+34,562/2 = 33,281 or Rs 33,000.

Average cost per hectare between 2005 to 2020

Costs:

1. Cost of drilling borewell with casing pipe/digging open well with parapet wall.
   a. Cost in 1989 Rs 7,063
   b. Cost in 2005 @4% rise of cost per annum
      $7{,}063 \times (1+4/100)^{16} = 7{,}063 \times 2.03 =$ Rs 14,338
   c. Cost in 2020 @4% rise of cost per annum
      $14{,}338 \times (1+4/100)^{15} = 14{,}338 \times 1.95 =$ Rs 27,960.
   d The average cost of drilling borewell/digging open well in period 2005 to 2020 per annum per hectare =
      14,338+27,960/2 = 42,998/2 = 21,149 or Rs 21,000.
2. Motors and accessories
   a. Cost in 1989 Rs 14,062

b. Cost in 2005 @4% rise of cost per annum
$14,062 \times (1+4/100)^{16} = 14,062 \times 2.03 =$ Rs 28,546

c. Cost in 2020 @4% rise of cost per annum
$28,546 \times (1+4/100)^{15} = 28,546 \times 1.95 =$ Rs 55,665.

d. The average cost per annum per hectare in period 2005 to 2020
(28,546+55,665)/2 = 84,211/2 = 42,106 or Rs 42,000.

3. Cost of installing drip/sprinkler sets with accessories

a. Cost of sprinkler in 1989 Rs 10,875

b. Cost of installation of drip in 1989 Rs 13,437

c. Average cost of sprinkler/drip
(A+B)/2 = 10,875+13,437/2 = Rs 12,156

d. Cost in 2005 for sprinkler/drip
$12,156 \times (1+4/100)^{16} = 12,156 \times 2.03 =$ Rs 24,677

e. Cost in 2020
$24,677 \times (1+4/100)^{15} = 24,677 \times 1.95 =$ Rs 48,120

f. Average cost per hectare per annum for sprinkler/drip in the period 2005 to 2020.
24,677+48,120/2 = Rs 72797/2 or Rs 36,398 or Rs 36,000

Abstract of various cases of utilisation of groundwater with sprinkler/drip and the cost thereof per hectare

Case 1. New borewell/dug well

a. Drilling/digging well	Rs 21,000
b. Motor with accessories	Rs 42,000
c. Installing sprinkler/drip with accessories	Rs 36,000
d. Land development with drainage (OFD FDC)	Rs 10,000
Total	**Rs 1,09,000**

Case 2. Where well/bore well exists with motor and accessories

a. Cost of installing drip/sprinkler	Rs 36,000
b. Land development (repairs of OFDs and FDCs)	Rs 2,500
Total	**Rs 38,500**

Case 3. Where well exists without motors

a. Cost of installing motor and accessories	Rs 42,000
b. Cost of installing sprinkler/drip	Rs 36,000
c. Land development (repairs of OFDs and FDCs)	Rs 2,500
Total	**Rs 80,500**

Appendix 8

White Paper on South African Water Policy with Comments

Water in our Lives

According to Bill of Rights of Constitution of South Africa, Section 27 (b); every one has the right to have access to water. The paper wants water to reach into a network reaching every individual. In other words, water gathered and stored since the beginning of time in layers of granite and rock, in the embrace of dams, the ribbons of rock, ribbons of rivers will one day, unheralded, modestly, easily flow out to every South African who turns a tap.

South Africa's water law comes out of a history of conquest and expansion. The colonial law makers, tried to use rules of the well watered colonising countries of Europe in the dry and variable climate of Southern Africa. They harnessed the law, and water in the interest of a dominant class and group which had privileged access to land and economic power.

The constitution therefore, demands a review of the situation, on the basis of fairness and equity, values which are enshrined as cornerstones of their new society. Further, growing population and meeting the demands of disadvantaged majority for water, which is a limited resource is a challenge, which they have to meet.

The present use of the resource, is not giving the social, economic and environmental benefits it should give. Building dams on rivers have a limit, since replenishing water beyond the water flow capacity of rivers is as good as, borrowing money by a small budget household, which it cannot afford to repay. Water conservation programmes may be better investments than investment in new dams, etc. Conservation programmes may both increase water supply by for instance, controlling and use practices and manage demand (e.g., application of appropriate tariffs).

This is considered a significant challenge particularly because rainfall is uneven in time and space, where the areas of highest rainfall are far from the industrial and urban heartland and from areas of rural poverty; where crippling droughts and devastating floods repeatedly wreck vengeance and where water resources are inequitably distributed and sometimes inappropriately used.

In view of the fact, South Africa has shown the world that peace can be created out of conflict and these national values of reconciliation, reconstruction and development will be reflected in equitable sharing of water and appropriate use of the same.

Summary of Policy Approaches

In view of colonisation and water mostly being used by dominant groups in the past, a review of such privileges in water sharing on the basis of fairness and equity is called for.

There is a limit to the development of new dam and water transfers which can be affected. Therefore, present use of water is often wasteful and inefficient resulting in not getting benefits that should accrue from investments made. Water conservation might be a better investment than new dams. New approaches are needed for water management.

Process of Policy

The policy development process has been assisted by the support and involvement of officials of other countries and international organisations.

Key Proposals

Some of the key proposals which will guide water management in South Africa in the future are that:

1. The most important objective is to promote the well-being of all South Africans, present and future.
2. In view of historical disparities, in sharing water, the new national law will recognise the need for a period of adjustment, which in some cases will last years, but provisions for interim arrangement will be made.
3. The new approach put in place, will be sensitive to particular problems faced by each sector. Farmers will be helped to adjust; mines and manufacturing industry will be encouraged to promote their own programmes to meet standards which will be set, monitored and enforced by government; conservation programmes are being started to enable local governments and domestic users to meet their obligations.

4. The objective in relation to our neighbours is the same as it is within South Africa's border, to ensure that we adjust to the pressures and demands of the future through cooperation, not conflict, in harmony with our common development.
5. These objectives and approaches are essential if we are to achieve the national goal of making sure that there will always be some water, for all who need it, contributing towards growing prosperity and equity in our land.

The Department of Water Affairs and Forestry whose staffs have committed themselves to ensuring: Some For All For Ever, which sums up goals of:

- Access to a limited resource (some)
- On an equitable basis (for all)
- In a sustainable manner (for ever)

The New South African Context

The constitution of South Africa, commits itself to establishing a society based on democratic values, social justice and fundamental human rights through among other things improving the quality of life of all citizens and freeing the potential of all persons. It also acknowledges a collective commitment to remedy the injustices and heal the divisions of the past.

Although the constitution guarantees certain protection in respect of property, there are different ways in which a person's property rights can be interfered with, by the state. The property rights question cannot be understood without looking at the important provisions of the constitution, which guarantees every person the right to access sufficient water and food, and to health care services. This promises every child right to, amongst other things, basic nutrition and health care services. Access to sufficient affordable water should be seen as part of primary health care services. In other words, in course of time the riparian rights which the colonisers secured by occupying lands in upper reaches of streams have to go.

Apartheid was an inefficient spoils system under which the distribution of water use was racially biased, and access to water and benefits from its use was a privilege of those with access to land, and political and economic power. In the context of reform of water law, the right to equality requires equitable access by all South African to, and benefit from nation's water resources and an end to discrimination with regard to access to water on the basis of race, class or gender.

The reform of water law must therefore, put in place arrangements to ensure, amongst other things, that all South Africans gain access to water, to meet basic domestic needs, the reallocation of existing water uses – to improve the optimum and equitable use of water – is therefore constitutionally valid, this is in line with international developments, which have increased role of the state as public trustee and natural resources.

Cooperative Governance: Like in India water is a national and also provincial subject. But distribution of water, maintenance of sanitation is a municipal subject. Therefore, the White Paper emphasises that it is the duty of both national and provincial governments to make sure that municipalities are effectively performing their functions including provision of water supplies and sanitation services and to assist them to achieve the goal.

Water and South Africa's Development Vision

The achievement of South Africa's development vision will be possible if water resources are managed in a way, which is sensitive to and supportive of many demands which we place upon them.

Uses of water are as under:

1) On a priority basis for domestic consumption and where water borne sewerage is installed to transport human waste.
2) For making agriculture viable. Hence, it is considered necessary that land reforms programme must be harmonised with programmes to ensure equitable access to water if land is to be made productive.
3) Forestry development creates jobs and incomes in rural areas and forest provides the raw material for an important industry in which South Africa is a leader, the water needs of forestry have to be balanced with those of other uses.
4) Of many other demands, mining, manufacturing and power generation together use about a quarter as is consumed by agriculture. Yet, the value they add and the jobs they create per kilolitre of water far outstrip those of agriculture and forestry. This does not mean that manufacturing industry is more important – agriculture plays a vital role in supporting rural communities. It does, however, suggest that it would not be in the interest of national prosperity to unnecessarily constrain industries to water.
5) Most water uses also impact on the environment and the cost of this must be accounted for in assessed the economic benefits of alternative water users and development. To sustain the established users of water, the natural resource base must be suitably protected. However, within

a safeguarded natural environment, the water available to support tourism and recreation also has potential for job creation.

A Scare and Sensitive Resource

South Africa is an arid country with rainfall less that the world average very unevenly distributed across the country. It has 1,200 kilolitres of available fresh water for each person each year at the present population of 42 million. SA is at the threshold of water crisis. In a few years population growth will take South Africa below the level. SA already has less water per person than countries considered to be much drier, such as Namibia and Botswana.

Another measure of water availability is the amount of water resource already being used in South Africa. SA uses more than half of the total water that they can afford to use, while arid Namibia and Botswana use 5%-10% of their available water.

Many of the largest and fastest growing water users for historical reasons, are found at the beginning of small erratic streams, rather than at the end of large reliable rivers. As a consequence the waste from human and economic activity is concentrated where it has to meet severe impact. The regions where water is still relatively plentiful are often those where nature of the land or other factors limit broader socio-economic development. Another limitation is South Africa's major river systems, such as Orange, Limpope and Komate are shared with neighbouring countries.

The unconventional source of water available and used in small projects in desalination of sea water is highly cost intensive. Hence not water but financial resources impose the final constraint on our development.

Water resource cannot be managed in isolation from other natural resources. Water availability is governed by the water cycle, in which rain falls from clouds, flows over the land or sucks through the ground, where it may be stored as groundwater in underground aquifers, and finally flows though rivers, lakes and dams towards the sea. Evaporation from surface water and the transpiration of plants and trees feed the clouds and the cycle continues.

The use of land then has a major impact on water resources. Similarly, air pollution can gravely affect water quality. The ways we use or abuse our rivers has an effect on estuaries and ocean around our coast. Within water resource itself, there are complex interactions between water and the sediments, banks, animals, plants and microbes in rivers, dam and wetlands, which must be taken into account in water management. Finally, human activities are beginning to have a noticeable impact on our climate which could affect the amount and distribution of rainfall and rates of evaporation, all of which must be taken into account in our water resource policy.

The complexity of all these interactions calls for a complex integrated approach to management.

The Socio-economic Context: Water policy must be appropriate to the social and economic context in which it is implemented. South Africa is worst of in social indicators of comparable middle income countries.

In terms of income distributions SA is one of the most unequal countries in the world. At least 32% of people are unemployed. As a result of apartheid, deprivation and poverty, Africans have twice the unemployment of coloureds, three times that of Indians and ten times that of Whites. Africans also comprise nearly 95% of South Africa's poor. Poverty is concentrated in rural areas where nearly 75% of South Africa's poor live. 45% of SAs poor are children. It affects mostly women and children, particularly women headed households, gradually in rural and peri-urban areas. African women in these areas have no choice but to walk long distance to collect water, a heavy burden which directly impacts on their health and incomes. Consequently, children also are victims of disease related to poor sanitation and the lack of clean water.

It is difficult to come out of this web of poverty inequality, lack of education, etc., government itself with its limited resources can cover only 15% of what is required to achieve modest improvement in living standards. The scale of deprivation is clearly visible in the lack of water services with between 12 and 14 million without access to safe water and over 20 million without adequate sanitation out of 42 million population.

Water Reconstruction and Development: The Reconstruction and Development Programme (RDP) the core of South Africa's development vision emphasises that growth and development are not opposing goals but essential pillars of a common strategy. It states that without an improvement in quality of life of the majority of South Africans the political conditions for growth will not exist and that without growth, the economic conditions for an improved quality of life cannot be created.

Within the framework, the key programmes of RDP are:

- Meeting basic needs
- Developing human resources
- Building the economy
- Democratising the state and society.

The vision of South Africa is not about houses, services and education only. It is of a country where people have opportunities, to develop their skills and opportunities to use them productively to work and earn an income with which they can at least meet their basic needs. It is a vision where, because there are opportunities, people can live at peace with one another, in dignity and security, where because of wise management, the environment in which people live, work hard and relax is healthy and pleasant and can be kept so.

The key principles of the vision have been restated in the Growth, Employment, and Redistribution (GEAR) macro-economic strategy. It thus remains an important guide to action.

The GEAR aims to boost economic growth by lowering protective barriers in a number of industrial sectors, promoting small and medium size industry and greater integration with SADC countries as well as internationally competitive manufacturing industry. It emphasises that South Africa cannot grow merely through exploitation of crude natural resources, which applies as much to water as to more traditional area of minerals.

To address the needs of the rural poor, GEAR focuses on land reforms and associated agricultural development and on provision of infrastructure notably water. Investment in public infrastructure is an important focus, both to generate jobs and improve quality of life and also improve the productivity of the economy. Key success factors in this area include the organisation of service provisions in a manner which recovers their cost and facilitates the use of capital from the private sector.

The Development Vision for Water

Given the multiple and sometimes competing uses of water, the Reconstruction and Development Programme (RDP) highlighted the need for integrated management, which would ensure access to water for growing sectors of economy and not unnecessarily constrain economic development but equally, not damage the natural resource from which water was received. It emphasised the importance of ensuring that our neighbours have access to their legitimate share of the resource. The law must thus address the management of water for, and sharing water between, all these uses before it addresses the individual uses themselves.

Water management and water law in South Africa is thus at crossroads not just because there is a new government with new values, and new objectives but because a new reality has to be addressed. While resources were plentiful, the task was simply to harness them. Dams, pumping stations and pipelines were built to store flood water for use in periods of drought and to redistribute it to supply the activities and areas where it was most needed which, according to policies of the time, was in white South Africa.

This historic focus of water management has to change. Since much of accessible resource has been developed (and there is less and less untapped flood water reliable enough to be worth storing) the task is increasingly to manage within the constraints that are given to us by nature. This transition requires new legal instruments. Thus, the riparian principle which previously guided water allocation was an effective instrument of apartheid state to encourage and assist white land owners to use water to develop their land and an agriculturally-based economy. Government's policy is now to promote growth of industry and to increase jobs in areas such as tourism as well as greater equity in society.

The water management system and the law which underpins it must now be adapted to reflect these priorities and to meet the needs of consumers who are more productive in their use of water. This should be done in a way which remains supportive of agricultural economy, upon which many South Africans will continue to depend, for many years in future. Above all, it should be done in a way which is supportative of the imperatives of the constitution, which promotes equity and opportunity for all South Africans, protects their reasonable rights and upon whom it places reasonable demands.

In the years and decades to come, the same amount of water will have to be shared between a growing number of users and demands of their developing society. The manner in which this is done will determine the success of South Africa as a society. The realities of water are shared by all. The dire warnings of the past which suggested that within thirty years, the shortage of water would paralyse South Africa's development were wrong.

The challenge of the twenty-first century water management is to ensure that the society develops in a way that can function successfully, within constraints of the resource base. It is to treat the development use and protection of water as a common endeavour in the interest of all in the spirit of a new patriotism rather than as a series of conflicts between different groups. It is in this spirit that the new water law will be written.

Comments

The above White Paper brings out certain hard facts pertaining to an economy in which the available water has largely been used by the apartheid state to encourage White land owners for development of their land agriculturally.

Although ownership of land substantially vests with the Whites but still a number of other South Africans are also dependent on agricultural economy thereby it is necessary to continue to give just required quantities of water for the survival and success of agricultural economy. But at the same time, in order to provide more jobs to South Africans industrial development using local mineral resources and services, etc., are also to be developed. Towards this also there is need of water, in addition the habitats of the non-white South Africans have been supplied insufficient water for drinking and sanitation facilities. Towards this also there is need of water. The White Paper makes it amply clear that all these have to be managed within the limited quantity of water which South Africa gets every year as its right without ignoring the rights of neighbouring countries. In addition, it is also made clear in the paper that storage of flood water by constructing dams, pumping stations, etc., with this limited water has been substantially done already and very little scope for further harnessing of water is left to that country. In this situation the South African government's white paper speaks of formulation of a law towards meeting all their needs. No doubt, governmental legislation will assist various sections of the South African society. In addition to legislation, and in view of the views expressed in this study elsewhere above for utilising water in India it would be helpful for South Africa to reinforce their legal system envisaged in the White Paper, with a water supply system using drips and sprinklers universally for agriculture throughout the country. This supply system would substantially resolve the problem of supplying limited water for their multifarious needs. Conversely, although we have envisaged in this study, the supply of water for agriculture using drip and sprinkler for our agricultural needs so that substantial quantities of water are available for drinking water, sanitation, industrial and other purpose. In this study the availability of water for purposes of other than agriculture has been quantified for the year ending with 2020 and 2050. In fact, the South African situation of the Whites dominating land in upper reaches of natural water supply systems and claiming riparian rights for their agriculture is similar to our powerful/rich cultivators purchasing lands nearer the upper reaches of our major/medium irrigation canal systems and violating the law by cultivating heavy water duty consuming crops like paddy and sugarcane even in areas where the law clearly envisages growing of low water duty crops like jowar, bajra cotton, etc., while the White Paper of South Africa also has envisaged just principles for formulation of a law of equitable distribution of water. In our case we have a law which allows water to reach lands at long distances at the tail end of the canal systems, but it is not being enforced by sheer influence and social power of the farmers at the upper reaches. In any case the thesis in this paper of universally supplying water for agriculture through the usage of micro-hydel system stands very valid both in the Indian and South African context.

List of Acronyms

USSR	Union of Soviet Socialist Republics
USA	United States of America
GOI	Government of India
MMI	Major and Medium Irrigation
WUA	Water Users' Association
EIA	Environmental Impact Assessment
NGO	Non-Governmental Organisations
R&D	Research and Development
DPAP	Drought Prone Area Programme
DDP	Desert Development Programme
NWDPRA	National Watershed Development Project for Rainfed Areas
IWDP	Integrated Watershed Development Programme
RWA	Residents Welfare Association
UN	United Nations
PWD	Public Works Department
FYP	Five Year Plan
MOA	Ministry of Agriculture
CADA	Command Area Development Authority
FMI	Flood/Flow Method of Irrigation
FIC	Field Irrigation Channels
FDC	Field Drainage Channels
OFD	On Farm Development
SMI	Sprinkler Method of Irrigation
DMI	Drip Method of Irrigation

RBI	Reserve Bank of India
RIL	Reliance Industries Limited
NREGS	National Rural Employment Guarantee Scheme
DLC	Distributory Level Committee
NCIWRD	National Commission on Integrated Water Resources Development
KWDT	Krishna Water Disputes Tribunal

References

1. Agricultural Finance Corperation, Bombay; Financing Drip Irrigation Schemes in Tamil Nadu: A feasibility Report, Prepared for Indian Petro Chemicals Corporation, Baroda.
2. Agricultural Finance Consultants Limited (formerly Agricultural Finance Corporation Ltd.), Bombay; Drip Irrigation Schemes for Community Wells in Tamil Nadu: A Feasibility Report Prepared for Government of Tamil Nadu, Madras, August 1989.
3. Agricultural Finance Corporation, Bombay; Financing Drip Irrigation Schemes in Bihar: A Feasibility Report Prepared for Indian Petro Chemicals Corporation Limited, Vododara (Gujarat), 1988.
4. Agricultural Finance Corporation Ltd., Mumbai, Northern Regional Office, New Delhi-October; Evaluation of Drip Irrigation Systems, sponsored by Department of Agricultural and Cooperation, and National Committee on use of plastic in agriculture, Ministry of Agriculture, Government of India, 1998.
5. Agricultural Finance Consultants (formerly Agricultural Finance Corporation Ltd.), Bombay, January 1989; Comprehensive Landuse Management Project, Hakanhal Mandal, Bellary District: A Feasibility Report prepared for Government of Karnataka, January 1989.
6. Centre for Science and Environment; State of India's Environment 4 A Citizen Report, Dying wisdom – Rise, Fall and Potential of India's Traditional Water Harvesting Systems.
7. Development of Irrigation Potential (cumulative) through Plans (Annexure 8.1.2 X Five Year Plan, GOI).

8. Firodoa, Arun; 'Cows are for Ever, Methane Gas, the Answer to Oil Imports'; The Times of India, 8 December 2004.

9. Government of Karnataka; Planning Department (PFR Division); Inter State Economic Indicators, May 2004.

10. Government of Karnataka, Revenue Reforms Commission, First Report, Volume I, November 2003.

11. Government of Karnataka, Revenue Reforms Commission, Final Report, February 2004.

12. Government of Karnataka; Comprehensive Land Use Management Project.

13. Government of India, Planning Commission; Eleventh Five Year Plan 2007-12.

14. 'Irrigation Equipment', Agriculture and Industries Survey, Volume 14, Issue No. 8, 2004.

15. Interlinking of Rivers, Ministry of Water Resources, Government of India, New Delhi, 2003 – Inter-basin Water Transfer Proposals - Headed by Shri Suresh T. Prabhu

16. Newson, Malcolm; Land, Water and Development: Sustainable Management of River Basins.

17. Srinivasan, T.M.; Irrigation and Water Supply in South India 200 BC–1600 AD.

18. White Paper on Water Policy-South Africa, 30 April 1977.

Index